COPING WITH A MID-LIFE CRISIS

DR DEREK MILNE (PhD) is a clinical psychologist working full-time for the UK's National Health Service (NHS). He is based at Newcastle University, where he is Director of the Doctorate in Clinical Psychology, a training programme preparing psychologists for work in the NHS. A Fellow of the British Psychological Society, Dr Milne has written several self-help books as well as many professional books and scientific papers. A major theme in his work is how people handle the stress of everyday life, so *Coping with a Mid-life Crisis* continues this interest.

# Overcoming Common Problems Series

*Selected titles*
A full list of titles is available from Sheldon Press,
1 Marylebone Road, London NW1 4DU, and on our website at
www.sheldonpress.co.uk

**Assertiveness: Step by Step**
Dr Windy Dryden and Daniel Constantinou

**Body Language at Work**
Mary Hartley

**The Cancer Guide for Men**
Helen Beare and Neil Priddy

**The Candida Diet Book**
Karen Brody

**The Chronic Fatigue Healing Diet**
Christine Craggs-Hinton

**Cider Vinegar**
Margaret Hills

**Comfort for Depression**
Janet Horwood

**Confidence Works**
Gladeana McMahon

**Coping Successfully with Hay Fever**
Dr Robert Youngson

**Coping Successfully with Pain**
Neville Shone

**Coping Successfully with Panic Attacks**
Shirley Trickett

**Coping Successfully with Prostate Cancer**
Dr Tom Smith

**Coping Successfully with Prostate Problems**
Rosy Reynolds

**Coping Successfully with RSI**
Maggie Black and Penny Gray

**Coping Successfully with Your Hiatus Hernia**
Dr Tom Smith

**Coping with Alopecia**
Dr Nigel Hunt and Dr Sue McHale

**Coping with Anxiety and Depression**
Shirley Trickett

**Coping with Blushing**
Dr Robert Edelmann

**Coping with Bronchitis and Emphysema**
Dr Tom Smith

**Coping with Candida**
Shirley Trickett

**Coping with Childhood Asthma**
Jill Eckersley

**Coping with Chronic Fatigue**
Trudie Chalder

**Coping with Coeliac Disease**
Karen Brody

**Coping with Cystitis**
Caroline Clayton

**Coping with Depression and Elation**
Dr Patrick McKeon

**Coping with Down's Syndrome**
Fiona Marshall

**Coping with Dyspraxia**
Jill Eckersley

**Coping with Eczema**
Dr Robert Youngson

**Coping with Endometriosis**
Jo Mears

**Coping with Epilepsy**
Fiona Marshall and
Dr Pamela Crawford

**Coping with Fibroids**
Mary-Claire Mason

**Coping with Gallstones**
Dr Joan Gomez

**Coping with Gout**
Christine Craggs-Hinton

**Coping with a Hernia**
Dr David Delvin

**Coping with Incontinence**
Dr Joan Gomez

**Coping with Long-Term Illness**
Barbara Baker

**Coping with the Menopause**
Janet Horwood

**Coping with a Mid-life Crisis**
Derek Milne

**Coping with Polycystic Ovary Syndrome**
Christine Craggs-Hinton

**Coping with Psoriasis**
Professor Ronald Marks

# Overcoming Common Problems Series

# Overcoming Common Problems Series

**Is HRT Right for You?**
Dr Anne MacGregor

**Letting Go of Anxiety and Depression**
Dr Windy Dryden

**Lifting Depression the Balanced Way**
Dr Lindsay Corrie

**Living with Asthma**
Dr Robert Youngson

**Living with Autism**
Fiona Marshall

**Living with Crohn's Disease**
Dr Joan Gomez

**Living with Diabetes**
Dr Joan Gomez

**Living with Fibromyalgia**
Christine Craggs-Hinton

**Living with Grief**
Dr Tony Lake

**Living with Heart Disease**
Victor Marks, Dr Monica Lewis and
Dr Gerald Lewis

**Living with High Blood Pressure**
Dr Tom Smith

**Living with Hughes Syndrome**
Triona Holden

**Living with Nut Allergies**
Karen Evennett

**Living with Osteoarthritis**
Dr Patricia Gilbert

**Living with Osteoporosis**
Dr Joan Gomez

**Living with Ulcerative Colitis**
Peter Cartwright

**Losing a Child**
Linda Hurcombe

**Make Up or Break Up: Making the Most of Your Marriage**
Mary Williams

**Making Friends with Your Stepchildren**
Rosemary Wells

**Motor Neurone Disease – A Family Affair**
Dr David Oliver

**Overcoming Anger**
Dr Windy Dryden

**Overcoming Anxiety**
Dr Windy Dryden

**Overcoming Back Pain**
Dr Tom Smith

**Overcoming Depression**
Dr Windy Dryden and Sarah Opie

**Overcoming Guilt**
Dr Windy Dryden

**Overcoming Impotence**
Mary Williams

**Overcoming Jealousy**
Dr Windy Dryden

**Overcoming Procrastination**
Dr Windy Dryden

**Overcoming Shame**
Dr Windy Dryden

**Overcoming Your Addictions**
Dr Windy Dryden and
Dr Walter Matweychuk

**The Parkinson's Disease Handbook**
Dr Richard Godwin-Austen

**The PMS Diet Book**
Karen Evennett

**Rheumatoid Arthritis**
Mary-Claire Mason and Dr Elaine Smith

**The Self-Esteem Journal**
Alison Waines

**Shift Your Thinking, Change Your Life**
Mo Shapiro

**Stress and Depression in Children and Teenagers**
Vicky Maud

**Stress at Work**
Mary Hartley

**Ten Steps to Positive Living**
Dr Windy Dryden

**Think Your Way to Happiness**
Dr Windy Dryden and Jack Gordon

**The Traveller's Good Health Guide**
Ted Lankester

**Understanding Obsessions and Compulsions**
Dr Frank Tallis

**Understanding Sex and Relationships**
Rosemary Stones

**When Someone You Love Has Depression**
Barbara Baker

**Work–Life Balance**
Gordon and Ronni Lamont

**Your Man's Health**
Fiona Marshall

**Overcoming Common Problems**

# Coping with a Mid-life Crisis

## Derek Milne

First published in Great Britain in 2004 by
Sheldon Press
1 Marylebone Road
London NW1 4DU

*British Library Cataloguing-in-Publication Data*

A catalogue record for this book is available from the British Library

ISBN 0–85969–894–7

1 3 5 7 9 10 8 6 4 2

Typeset by Deltatype Ltd, Birkenhead, Merseyside
Printed in Great Britain at Ashford Colour Press

# Contents

# Acknowledgements

I would like to thank some friends and colleagues for their valuable comments on early drafts of the book (Ian James, Jacqui Rodgers, Julie Fisher and Marsha Jordyn), Lynne Henry for her helpful literature searches, those anonymous allies who provided me with their personal stories (they know who they are), editor Liz Marsh for her gentle guidance, Linda Crosby for copy-editing, and Helen Taylor for preparing the book. My daughter, Kirsty, is thanked for her unstinting belief and selfless support. But most of all, a huge thank you to my partner Janette Little, for everything.

# Introduction

Development is fluid and it is never too late for changes to take place.

(Rutter, 1978)

We humans have enormous potential, but achieving it is a mighty struggle. Ever since Darwin's theory of evolution there has been a clear recognition of the 'struggle for existence'. Although the raw 'struggle for existence' of pre-history may be over, the struggle for happiness that we all face today lies in coping successfully with the demands that our current world places upon us – from the minor hassles of daily existence to the major life events. Our 'existence' is defined by the way that we make use of our resources – especially our coping ability – to adapt to (or change) our circumstances, in order to develop. Therefore, adapting to our life circumstances can be seen as a fundamental human task, determining whether we end up feeling overwhelmed by a mid-life crisis or able to rise above it, with renewed confidence and greater personal happiness. Our development is built on such transitions.

## A particularly special period of life

The struggle to cope with the mid-life crisis is unique and especially taxing – researchers report that there is something particularly challenging about this transitional period. Statistically, the greatest rise in the number of suicides, major illnesses, accidents, psychiatric hospital admissions, depressions and abuses of alcohol take place between the ages of 40 and 50. Such figures highlight the struggle many seem to have in adapting to the circumstances of their mid-life. Some believe that this is partly because of the peculiar pressure that comes from being at our most powerful publicly (e.g. in terms of expertise, prestige, status, income), while privately beginning to feel a distinct weakening, as our physical selves begin their unmistakable decline. Although many report that these middle years are their 'golden period', others clearly struggle with the experience of being 'powerful' and 'powerless' at the same time. Whatever the cause, this contrast is usually strong and marks a significant passage of time, one that typically also sees changes at home (e.g. the 'empty nest'), at work (e.g. a career may plateau or abruptly end), and in terms of our social world (e.g. becoming a carer for an ailing parent). Psychologically there is, then, a heightened awareness of the passage of time, of what might have been, and of the increasingly limited scope to make things happen in the future. And behind this powerlessness is a much sharper view of the inevitability of our death, and the increasingly urgent search for a meaning to our existence.

## The structure of this book

In the next chapter, I will place this special crisis in its personal and social context: in other words, we cannot hope to understand ourselves and what is happening to us without filling in the background and the various factors – such as our personality and personal history – that inevitably surround and provide the basis for a crisis. To make this context or backdrop as clear as possible, I will draw an explicit parallel between our lives and the theatre. That is, I will make a link between how we have a 'persona' (i.e. the part we play) on the 'stage' of life that consists of a 'set', other 'players', and the 'acting out' of a 'story'. Next, I go on to ask some key questions about the mid-life crisis itself – such as what exactly it is, whether it is special in some way and, if so, what makes it special? I will show how it is unlike the other transitions that we go through in life, as well as noting the ingredients that seem to go into making a crisis arise.

Following these introductory chapters, the heart of the book concentrates on our efforts to find a way through the crisis, and I will use the idea of 'coping' to cover our struggle for something more than mere adaptation and existence. Therefore, 'coping' as used in this book is not the same as the popular use of the term – just getting by, or keeping the wolf from the door (as in, 'How are things?' 'I'm just about coping'). Rather, I want to use the idea of 'coping' to capture the way that we each grapple with the demands of life, struggling and changing in order to achieve solutions and our own happiness. It is close to Darwin's idea of adaptation of a species to its environment, but with a couple of key differences. First, I will be concerned with the kind of adaptations that we can make in our own lifetime. Second, humans are especially good at changing the environment to ease the need for adaptation: unlike the dodo bird, we can change our physical world to avoid 'extinction', especially our social world (e.g. by emigrating or by moving back to live near our extended family). Adaptation for humans also depends critically on how we make sense of events, and of how we then respond given that understanding. The act of making sense of our situation places us in the driving seat, with the power to take control of things. Therefore, we need to understand our mid-life crisis before we can decide how best to respond to such stressors as divorce, caring for older family members, or unemployment at age 50-plus.

## A positive perspective

There are three basic ways of making sense of our situation and addressing these kinds of *stressors*: survival, recovery or thriving. In this book I will emphasize ways in which you can emerge from a mid-life crisis and thrive, even if there are times when all you feel you can do is survive to the next day. I also accept the need for a time to recover from difficult experiences. The goal, though, is *thriving*, and I believe that we do this best when we view our current crisis as a time of growth and personal change. Another reason to be optimistic is that we know that there *are* ways of coping successfully with crises. From these ways of coping come transition and development – so there is good reason to believe that a mid-life crisis can lead to greater personal happiness.

My own version of this transition is partly drawn from my experience as a human being who has experienced at least some aspects of the mid-life crisis; but it also comes from 20 years as a therapist, trying to help other adults to cope more successfully. My advice draws too on the extensive scientific and popular literature in this field. Lastly, I will be passing on important examples from the experiences of three people who have struggled through their own life crises, three 'personal stories' that run through this book.

The coping strategies that tend to work best will be set out in detail, and are at times contrasted with those strategies that are liable to fail. The emphasis is on spelling out and celebrating our ability to manage the everyday 'struggle for existence' and to grow from it. Indeed, it will be argued that the struggle brings benefits that might otherwise be absent from our lives. As demonstrated in the quote at the beginning of this Introduction, the crisis can be a stimulus to our further development – and this can go on indefinitely.

## *The benefits to be gained from this approach*

Good coping strategies also tend to lead to a sense of being in control, so that a kind of 'mastery' of the crisis can develop, and this phase of the coping cycle represents the final part of the book. However, there is an ongoing need to develop both our understanding and our coping strategies. In other words, coping needs to be viewed as part of an endless cycle or a long journey, a bit like the demands of sailing the seven seas. During this voyage there may well be times of comfort and great progress, but after periods of calm there are often some stormy seas. At such times it is important to draw on what we – and others – have learnt from earlier life crises or transitions; in this way, we can develop more confidence and control, reaping greater benefits and satisfaction from the 'second half' of our life. This analogy led to the 'seven Cs' that form the chapters.

If you have experienced a mid-life crisis – or if you are now experiencing one – this book will therefore offer you some clarity as to what is going on, tips on coping, and comfort. It will do this by identifying the particular stressors of the mid-life crisis, and also by showing how the unpleasant – and at times puzzling – aspects of the mid-life crisis can be better understood. Comfort can also come from realizing that these distressing experiences have been shared by others, many of whom have found ways of resolving their mid-life crisis successfully. Therefore, to help you to sense that you are not alone in your struggle, and to offer some clear examples of coping successfully, the experiences of the three people mentioned earlier run through the book. They are Mike, a successful and previously self-assured professional, who was astounded by his mid-life crisis; Teena, also previously confident and seemingly safe from such a personal crisis in her happy marriage; and John, more of a sensitive type – and so perhaps more akin to the popular idea of the kind of person who would be 'at risk' of a mid-life crisis. Each of these personal stories highlights different life events and coping challenges – including the perspective that travel can bring to one's life; the shocking realization that things cannot go on as they are any longer; and the difficulty of making changes when everyone around you is trying to convince you that all is well. (Note: These stories are true ones, and told here with the permission of these individuals; the details have only been altered in unimportant ways, to protect the anonymity of those concerned.)

In addition to the comfort that I believe will come from realizing that you are not alone, your confidence in dealing with these kinds of stressful experiences should also grow. This will result from studying the successful ways of coping that others, such as Mike, Teena and John, have used. These coping strategies will be presented in an optimistic and practical way. Additional features of the book that are designed to make the material even more useful are 'Points to Ponder' and 'Things to Try' (in order to change and improve your coping). The 'Points to Ponder' are a few central questions to encourage your personal reflection on the material covered in individual chapters, and to help you to consider possible ways forward. Some ideas for personal change, in the form of things you might like to try, accompany the middle chapters on coping strategies. At the back of the book, you will find suggestions for further reading; these offer a way of exploring each topic in more depth, if you so wish. Finally, the chapters are organized around a few major questions, with the material presented as a series of replies to these questions. This is to maximize the relevance of the text and to ease the accessing of the information that you find most important.

In summary, this book offers you a clear, factual, well-founded and uplifting account of the mid-life crisis, one that is interwoven with personal accounts from those who have been through it all and emerged from their voyage stronger and happier human beings. Drawing on current research and my experiences as a therapist and a teacher, I then outline several constructive ways of understanding and dealing with the crisis. As you will have realized by now, the emphasis throughout the book will be on practical and positive ways forward. The mid-life crisis may be demanding and difficult, but it is also an opportunity to redesign your life. This period in your middle years is thus a way of preparing you for the next episode in your personal 'struggle for existence' and also a springboard – helping you towards achieving your potential and greater personal happiness.

# 1

## Context for your crisis

All the world's a stage, and all the men and women merely players: they have their exits and their entrances; and one man in his time plays many parts, his acts being seven ages.

(William Shakespeare, *As You Like It*)

The 'struggle for existence' that Darwin emphasized in his writings always takes place within a particular context – a time, place and personally important 'space'. This context was for him a vital clue in terms of his theory of how we evolved. Likewise, it is hard to imagine a personal crisis taking place without some kind of significant context surrounding it, such as particular relationship problems or tricky transitions at home or work. We 'players' cannot act without our 'stage'.

Another link with his theories is the need to find our own ways of adapting to the particular circumstances in which we find ourselves. According to Darwin's view of evolution, it is the interaction between our own efforts to cope and our environment that allows for the personal adjustment, or the 'survival of the fittest'; and in this book, I will be trying to improve your 'fitness' so that you can survive, and even thrive, in your own particular context.

In this chapter, though, I am going to try to aid your coping efforts by first helping you to understand how your personality emerges from your childhood experiences. This vital part of your past shapes the 'part' you play on life's stage, including what you think, feel and do about your present crisis. As a result of the way we are, and of the context in which we exist, we all have some areas of strength – and also our share of weaknesses. These are called 'protective' and 'vulnerability' factors; protective factors include personal strengths, such as 'hardiness', and strengths that come from our context, such as the social support that we receive from others. (We will deal with 'vulnerability' factors a bit later on.) Lastly, we'll look at how our context includes a number of distinctive life periods, which tend to create particular tasks for the various phases (or 'acts') we play our part in throughout life. Shakespeare's quote above highlights his

1

belief that we each have seven phases or 'acts' on life's stage – a view shared by more recent commentators, as we'll see. A second point about Shakespeare's quote is that he seems to have viewed the environment – the stage of life – as crucial, a viewpoint shared by myself and many other researchers.

## What is the personal context?

One of the ways in which we can adapt successfully, then, is to take due account of the context in which our crisis is occurring. We should aim to be aware of who we are, and what is going on around us. To do this, we need to consider such questions as 'Why is it that I keep on making the same mistakes, getting caught up in the same old patterns?' and 'Why is this happening now?' These two questions get at those Darwinian notions of individual ways of coping within a specific context.

Within this chapter, these ways of coping will be considered in terms of our personalities and the other personal background factors that we each bring to the situation. This will help us to understand why we react as we do in particular contexts. The fact that we may react differently from others is not necessarily a problem. Indeed, according to Darwin's view, such variation between one person and another is essential for the success of the species. Some therefore believe that major transitions, such as the mid-life crisis, are things that are valuable experiences. In other words, they can be viewed as an indication of a 'fit personality'. In this sense, the mid-life crisis can be seen as an important and useful adaptation to a particular life context, for a particular person at a particular time. This brings in ideas such as the phases that we may go through during our life, and the tasks that we may be expected to tackle within our lifetime.

## Our personalities make us the 'players' we are

We each bring something different to the situations we find ourselves in. Sometimes an important life situation, such as the place where we are brought up, is nothing to do with us: we carry no responsibility for that part of our world. More typically, many of the situations that we find ourselves in can be seen as at least partly caused by us, whether we realize it or not; and research and clinical practice demonstrates that personal factors are usually partly responsible for our predicament. One example of this would be the way that somebody who is by nature an extrovert will tend to seek out the more stimulating social situations. Once in that situation, the extrovert will tend to increase the stimulation level still further. For this reason, understanding how our own personal make-up contributes to our context, and hence to our transition, is a vital part of dealing successfully with a mid-life crisis.

The most popular way of thinking about our 'make-up' is the idea of *personality*. This concept is derived from the ancient Greek word for the masks that actors of that period wore to indicate the particular character types that they were playing (from the Greek *persona*). Personality is usually defined as a tendency to act in particular ways, ones that make us distinctive or reveal 'who we are'. We think of someone as indicating their personality through the ways that they typically respond to people and situations. Humour often makes this link clear, as it depends on knowing the individual in order to be funny. Therefore in tackling your mid-life crisis, you will tend to show your own particular ways of dealing with the demands that this transition creates.

Personality is often thought of as a fairly fixed way of being and reacting to life (our 'disposition'), but clearly it also develops during our lives. If it were not possible to change the way that we respond to situations, then there would be little point in things like schools or training for a career. Self-help books, such as this one, would also be futile. But we *do* learn and adapt, helped or hindered by our personalities. It makes more sense, therefore, to think of personality as a fairly firm foundation for how we deal with our world. As we develop, we build on it a range of responses or coping strategies that we then use to deal with situations. Sometimes we discover that our personality is partly creating those situations, and also that it is making it hard to learn how to find fresh and effective ways of coping with them. As a result, a kind of 'vicious cycle' is set up, trapping us into recurring patterns of reacting to others. A quote from John illustrates this kind of process in relation to marital discord:

*Often I'd try to get my way with her by playing it cool, by being reserved or even disapproving. I wanted to let her know I wasn't*

3

*going to stand for it and that she was in the wrong. Unfortunately, this usually only served to make things worse, as she reacted by getting even more stand-offish and distant towards me. The atmosphere would get worse and worse, until usually there'd be an angry show-down, or we'd make up physically while half conscious in the middle of the night. I realized that neither of these solutions were actually much good, and that I rarely got my way. Still, I found it terribly hard to break this pattern, even though I often knew when it was repeating itself.*

Hopefully this book will help you to understand better how, like John, your personality shapes your life patterns and the situations it gets you into. These scenarios are called *lifetraps* (see below). Clearly, we need to find better ways of coping with these situations.

## Lifetraps keep us stuck in our roles

Most of us recognize that we have recurring, self-defeating patterns in our ways of dealing with people or situations. Typical examples are the relationships we feel drawn into – ones that repeat patterns of relating that happened in earlier relationships. Such patterns are known as lifetraps, and a most useful book, *Re-inventing Your Life* (see Further reading at the back of this book), describes the 11 most common ones. These lifetraps start in our childhood and shape our personality in powerful ways, influencing so much of how we develop. It starts with something that happened to us, such as feeling constantly criticized or belittled – perhaps by an older sibling or by parents. In this way, our basic needs are unmet or thwarted – such as our need for security and acceptance. This early pattern damages us by shaping the deeply held beliefs that we then develop – for example, that we just aren't good enough. Because of such experiences, we actually come to believe the relentless criticism and so form a view of ourselves as defective or inferior. Strangely enough, we may then try to re-create the same punishing situations as we go through life, where we again end up being put down or rejected. We do this to reach a relatively comfortable, familiar feeling or situation. Eventually we may realize that the pattern is repeating itself and try to get out of it. But after a while we slip back in again – a truly vicious cycle.

Some of the 11 lifetraps mentioned in *Re-inventing Your Life* are particularly relevant to the mid-life crisis. As outlined above, one trap is to feel 'defective' – that is, someone who is personally flawed. You may blame yourself for being someone who others – quite rightly in your eyes – cannot love or respect. A closely related lifetrap is that of 'failure', which tends to involve feeling inadequate. With this lifetrap you are always expecting others to find fault with you. In mid-life, such common lifetraps can be very destructive, as they are by now firmly rooted in your personality and so tend to cause you to keep getting into the same difficulties. For instance, if you believe that you are in some sense second-rate, then you are going to be particularly touchy about criticism or any form of rejection. In the past, you may have coped with this by working hard for approval, but as you enter a mid-life crisis your fragile self-belief may crumble under the pressure of your own intense life review. A vicious cycle may ensue, in which your coping strategies become half-hearted or desperate, failing to win you any approval and only worsening the downward spiral. And instead of trying to exit the situation (e.g. by taking some time off work), you may paradoxically intensify things – perhaps by going flat out on something that just might earn you extra approval. This is what I mean by a self-defeating pattern. There is a compulsion within us to repeat earlier patterns and to re-create earlier situations, even when we realize it's a case of 'here we go again'. This is partly because we feel a strange comfort or security in this uncomfortable, but familiar, state. It is also because we feel a deep need to tackle an old enemy, struggling to do our best to sort something out in our lives.

## *Our past explains so much*

Where does personality come from? Lifetraps are part of the answer, but there are a number of additional views, depending on which author you read. For instance, one view is that personality is largely something that comes from our parents: we inherit it through our genetic endowment. In this sense, personality is itself based on our 'temperament', something that our genetic blueprint dictates. This gives us our first personal foundation, our first pattern of reacting to events. We feel 'defective' because that's how our parents felt about themselves. An example of temperament would be the similar ways that children in the same family respond emotionally to the same event. The analogy that perhaps brings this home most clearly is to be found in dog breeding, where one expects to find terriers to be aggressive and spaniels to be friendly, for example. Studies in humans, looking at twins and adopted children, indicate that this explanation has some validity.

But different temperaments and the role of genetics do not provide a complete explanation for our personality. There is also clearly a place for experience and learning. The kinds of situations that we find ourselves in, including the physical and the social contexts, will create opportunities for us to adapt. Depending on the success of our efforts in adapting to particular situations (given our temperament and personality at that stage), we will learn to handle situations differently in the future. In this way, whatever is given to us genetically and that helps to make us unique or different is part of how we cope, and this approach is further strengthened by the way that we adapt to situations over time. In technical terms, there is a 'transaction' between who we are genetically, how we express that in the way that we interact with our world, and the physical social world that we inhabit.

Traditionally, some psychologists have thought that our personality is largely explained by some unconscious mental forces: our behaviour is shaped by processes beyond our awareness. This is a rather different view of things. Perhaps the best known of these forces or motives are the so-called 'defence mechanisms'. In this sense, without fully realizing it or planning it, people respond in characteristic ways to various situations, and these ways serve to protect an individual from unpleasant tensions or conflicts between the underlying or unconscious motives. An example would be 'rationalization', as in always having an answer or an excuse. The 'yes, but' reaction is a classic, whereby someone responds to a criticism by fleetingly acknowledging it (the 'yes' part), but moving swiftly on to reject the criticism with a string of impressive points (the 'but' part), preferably made with a contemptuous flourish. Therefore 'rationalization' is an intellectual or 'clever' way of protecting ourselves from criticism. In such a scenario, a person would also characteristically generate a number of reasons or arguments for why a particular criticism was not valid. This would protect them from experiencing the criticism, and thus also from being in some way threatened or diminished by a valid criticism. Patterns of this kind are sometimes strikingly evident in the way that people handle situations. At least, they're evident to others – being an unconscious behaviour, the person 'acting out the pattern' may lack any insight whatsoever. We can probably all think of members of our immediate family who will predictably respond to a situation in some such way, but when challenged will angrily deny doing so. By contrast, both the pattern and the lack of self-awareness or insight strike others most strongly. In extreme examples, such as the so-called 'personality disorders', the recurring patterns can develop into vicious cycles of action and reaction, and can reach the point where in-patient mental health care is necessary to protect the individual from themselves and from harming other people.

Whatever the reasons, people do differ in important ways, and a range of terms have been used to pick out these differences. Just as astrologers have star signs to set out these differences, so psychologists have spelt out our differences by using terms such as:

- Aggressive
- Sociable
- Stable
- Agreeable
- Extroverted
- Conscientious
- Neurotic
- Introverted
- Intelligent
- Dominant
- Hardy
- Tender-minded
- Suspicious

So how do we come to develop these characteristics? The simple answer surely lies in the coming together of our genes and our life experiences, within the context that we grow up and develop these features. It is an interaction between the individual and his or her environment. Even within the mother's womb, the developing infant will be subjected to an environment that may have adverse aspects –

such as the toxic effects of the mother's smoking or drinking habits on the foetus. In one study conducted in Hawaii, over 600 infants who had experienced complications in the womb, and also some adverse early rearing conditions (e.g. a physically impoverished home life), were followed up at the age of 30. The researchers found a clear link between adverse very early childhood experiences and a much greater likelihood of criminal involvement or divorce. However, the researchers found that personality factors, such as resilience and sociability, interacted with these early experiences, as did the coping strategies that these adults now used. This is a rather typical illustration of the way in which sometimes clear-cut physical events, such as problems within the womb or during early childhood, are linked to personality. In turn, this is related to how we adjust to situations over time (i.e. the coping strategies that we develop). Also relevant in this study was the finding that the social support that individuals received from the family played an important part as well. (I shall return later to the way in which these factors interact.)

As this study shows, adverse experiences of this kind may or may not dispose people towards negative experiences later in life. A crucial issue is the interaction between the individual's personality and their world. A second study in this field further illustrates this point, but this time the researchers worked *backwards* from a negative experience – in this case, depression – and looked at earlier experiences and circumstances that might explain it. They found that the quality of maternal care, as in highly over-protective parenting, was strongly related to particular personality styles, such as emotionality. Another very unfortunate part of early experience influencing later personality development relates to childhood abuse. Traumatic experiences of this kind early in life can damage personality, and so result in a range of problematic psychological symptoms. In turn, the emerging personality influences how we then *interpret* the abuse – for instance, perhaps as something for which we feel responsible. As a result, we may well experience shame for our involvement in the abuse. Other victims may blame the perpetrator, and consequently feel angry towards others. Depending on this interaction between personality and an early experience, people may take on different kinds of symptoms, or they may emerge from the most traumatic experiences with greater resilience or hardiness. Later on in life, though, when these individuals themselves become parents, there may remain some significant adverse consequences. In one study, low-income single mothers of pre-school children were interviewed regarding how well they thought they coped with their own children, relating this to how they felt that their own mothers had previously coped with rearing them. There was a strong relationship between what they had received as children and the care that they now provided as mothers. In particular, mothers who described maltreatment by their mothers, or experienced other negative childhood stressors, reported less success in their attempts to cope with their own children. They strongly related this to how they had experienced care-giving themselves as children. Also, those mothers who had negative experiences in their upbringing reported less confidence in their parenting abilities than did the other mothers in the study.

In this way, not only may our early experience shape our personality but later, as parents, our personalities may shape those of our children – and in turn their children. There is, then, both a genetic transmission from one generation to the next (as in temperament), and also a social transmission from one generation to the next. Personality also emerges from the social context within which those legacies arise, as in the way that our families use patterns of child care that are approved of by *significant others* (important people in our lives). In this sense, a parent who is already by nature prone to 'neuroticism' will have this anxious, worrying disposition exaggerated if in-laws or others share (or in a way endorse) this personality characteristic. As a result, it would not be surprising if the child grew up to share an anxious disposition to life.

It is clear, therefore, that temperament and personality play an important part in the way that we respond to events, including the mid-life crisis. It is also important to recognize that our personality is fairly resistant to change, and that our temperament is even more firmly fixed as a foundation of our being. This means that a sensible perspective to adopt in this situation is to be as aware as possible of the influences of our personalities and temperaments on how we are handling situations. Fortunately, there are ways in which we can use this awareness to help us to adjust. To return to the analogy of the theatre, although we may have a certain 'persona', we may none the less alter some of the theatrical set or backdrop, in order to better influence our own performance. We may even be able to adopt a different persona, especially if the context is sufficiently different. Another important point to make is that while temperament may serve as a foundation for personality, the way that we cope on a daily basis with the demands of life will also provide a major way of adapting. For this reason, the book places most emphasis on our personal coping strategies.

## *There are many ways of playing your part*

In the preceding section we noted some of the traditional terms that psychologists and others have used to try and describe personality. Some of these terms have grown in importance as a result of careful research, and the best-known examples are the so-called 'big five' personality factors. These are:

1 Extroversion
2 Agreeableness/friendliness
3 Conscientiousness
4 Emotional stability/neuroticism
5 Intellect/openness to experience

Each of these aspects of personality is thought of as varying along a continuum, from 'high' to 'low'. Because of this, each individual has a unique personality profile. In turn, each of these five personality factors is normally thought of as underpinning related personality features. For example, extroversion can be thought of as being responsible for the tendency to be warm, assertive, and having the ability to experience positive emotions. By contrast, neuroticism can be thought of as underlying such features as anxiety, self-consciousness and impulsiveness. However, it is important to think about these factors as simply being general descriptors for people, rather than applying closely to any one individual. We therefore require more specific terms in order to understand how each of us responds to particular demands, such as making a major life transition.

Far more helpful to our understanding of coping with a mid-life crisis are the following personality terms:

- Fighting spirit
- Denial

- Fatalism
- Self-esteem
- Hope and fantasy
- Self-destructiveness

Studies looking at these kinds of personal responses to situations indicate that they do in fact play a part in the way that people adjust. For instance, in one study of abused and normal children, followed up 14 years after an incident of abuse, the main distinguishing characteristics between the two groups were such things as high self-esteem and the use of hope and fantasy being observed in the non-abused youngsters. By contrast, factors that were associated with ongoing problems and poor adjustment were fatalism and self-destructiveness – more commonly seen in the abused group. Once again, the crucial issue is how these personality characteristics help the individual to adapt to stressful life circumstances. Sometimes a characteristic that is seemingly a disadvantage actually operates in order to protect somebody, at least in the short-term (e.g. using fantasy as a way of escaping from an unbearable stressor). In a positive sense, children who are exposed to abuse, or adults who are traumatized by the experience of war atrocities, may be helped to get through the distress by having an unrealistically high belief in their own importance or power. Such beliefs may protect them from the far more damaging realization of the opposite – namely, that we are all ultimately vulnerable and have a limited ability to prevent unfortunate events overtaking us, the clearest example being death.

This kind of finding has also been reported in relation to coping with major physical health stressors. Some studies of sufferers of serious illnesses have indicated that certain personality factors, such as a fighting spirit, seem to increase survival rates. By contrast, those who had the opposite reaction – of stoic acceptance or feeling helpless and hopeless – had worse outcomes, regardless of the initial physical problem. Those with a fighting spirit can be thought of as highly optimistic in their attitude to the illness, accompanied by a search for information to guide their coping. Denial, on the other hand, could be thought of as an active rejection of any information or evidence about their condition.

These kinds of personality characteristics are different from the 'big five' ones, such as 'extroversion', in that they are the daily, observable responses that we make to deal with stress. They also differ in being more under our control than the big personality factors. But they are probably based on our 'underlying' personality, which is in turn based on our temperament. In this way, it can be helpful to think of the ways we cope as the tip of an iceberg – the visible part of our make-up, and the part we can shape.

## Protective and vulnerability factors also play their part

As the above examples illustrate, the way we try to cope and our general disposition towards stress may make a huge difference to the way we respond, both psychologically and physically. Some reactions or dispositions may increase our vulnerability to stress. In a classic study of the social origins of depression, Brown and Harris (1978) found that women who did not have good social support, in terms of a close, confiding and trusted other (such as a husband or boyfriend), were much more likely to experience depression when exposed to any stress. Other vulnerability factors were having three or more children under 14 at home, and situations where the woman had lost her mother before the age of 11. The important point that Brown and Harris made, though, was that while these factors made an individual vulnerable, they did not necessarily *cause* depression. Therefore, they are best considered as 'risk factors' – things that increase the likelihood of a problem occurring, but that do not necessarily cause the problem. Other social factors, such as being unemployed, will further increase the individual's vulnerability. Personality factors are a further factor, affecting the likelihood of depression or other complications. For instance, those whose personality leads them to feel powerless and out of control in relation to their lives will be at greater risk. Again, one can trace some of these vulnerabilities to problems in childhood, problems that have not been satisfactorily resolved. If we again take the example of child sexual abuse, there is reason to believe that exposure to this severe form of stress may stop individuals developing normally. This may include the vital ability to form a strong and secure attachment to parental figures. In turn, this can interfere with the development of appropriate coping strategies that help people to make adjustments. In this way, some situations that require confidence and a sense of self-belief may be particularly difficult for individuals who are vulnerable in these areas. Mike illustrates this interaction between personality, current functioning and early experience:

> I always felt that my parents placed far more importance on running their business than they did on raising us kids. As a result, I don't think I was the only one who came to feel somewhat unimportant or devalued. It seemed as though the only way we could gain the attention and approval of Mum or Dad was to be successful at something. This led us children to be unusually successful in our jobs. However, when we talk about it, none of us is really content with our lot. We all feel a kind of disappointment and legacy from the fact that our parents didn't give us what is now called unconditional love. We reckon that we now try and find a proxy for love in the acceptance or approval that we get from others, as a result of being successful at work. In some ways this makes us vulnerable or susceptible to approval, as we work harder than most to try and gain it. There is also a sense in which we find ourselves repeating to our own children the emphasis on work that was so much a part of our own upbringing. It is really tough to try and break this vicious cycle.

As this hopefully illustrates, there is clearly a rich interaction between early childhood experience, personality and our attempts to cope in the present. Also, it illustrates how difficult it can be to break the patterns that have developed. This is partly because of inherited (and hence fixed) characteristics, such as our temperament, plus the early life experiences we have (e.g. the way our parents bring us up), or the way that we learn to adjust and adapt in our early lives.

## How 'hardiness' helps

However, it is surely true that when compensating for our vulnerabilities we develop some self-righting personality patterns. Very few individuals sink when the first large wave of a transition breaks on their shore. Far more commonly, individuals are like well-designed lifeboats, corks in the open sea: they may well get drenched, but none the less they survive. These qualities have been called such things as personal 'hardiness' or 'resilience'. Such capacities help people to overcome adversity, and even to go on and be productive and successful individuals (as Mike above). Again, resilience or hardiness is best understood as emerging from the same forces that shape vulnerability. Just as a parent may teach us to respond by caving in to stressors (e.g. by the way they themselves demonstrate this tendency to their children), so parents may teach their children to be hardy. This may come from a particular way of thinking about situations, so that these events can seem more manageable. One example is setting small, achievable goals and having a 'let's just get on with it' attitude. Also, parents may themselves demonstrate this resilience – modelling how to cope, even if they do not explicitly teach it. Whatever the process whereby such characteristics get passed on from parent to child, it is striking how widespread resilience or hardiness appear to be. Despite the many hardships of life, the great majority of people show the ability to manage demands and stressors and emerge from them cheerfully and successfully. We have an incredible ability to adapt to our context; and resilience is part of what makes us deal with stress and survive in life's jungle. Amazingly, the great majority of people emerge from this jungle all the better for the experience. They grow in self-belief, they become better parents or partners, and they make more valuable contributions to society. It is a stunning example of the way that we can adapt to our environment in ways that help us to grow.

## Developing a more 'positive' personality

It seems appropriate at this point to note the positive end of personality development. This growth is a result of these struggles for survival that we each go through in the jungle of life. The following list of features describes how a healthy personality typically looks:

1 An ability to accept oneself, others and the world in which we live (e.g. accepting shortcomings in others and not being ashamed of oneself or one's contribution to the world).

2 Accepting and dealing with reality (having a valid awareness and

understanding of unpleasant circumstances and trying to deal with them rather than avoid them).

3 Being spontaneous and natural (feeling comfortable expressing oneself).

4 Focusing on external things (having an interest in the issues of the day, and the ability to focus on practical tasks, rather than being absorbed in one's own problems).

5 Enjoying privacy (enjoying solitude more than most, possibly even appearing reserved or unruffled by events).

6 Remaining stable and secure (not being excessively dependent upon people and events for a sense of stability or well-being).

7 Appreciating life (having a fresh awareness of the wonders of even commonplace things and feeling a 'belongingness' with the rest of humanity).

## We also need to recognize our limits

However, although we clearly can make major adjustments and feel much better as a result, it is important to recognize limits to this process of change. The scientific evidence suggests increasingly strongly that personality sets definite limits on our flexibility. In other words, it appears that once we reach adulthood, our personalities remain fairly stable. There are no dramatic changes in our personalities as we age, and some would say that they even become more pronounced or entrenched in our make-up. This is important to recognize because it sets a definite limit on our ability to adapt to situations. All of this, though, is not to say that we should not attempt to change, but rather that we should adopt a more modest set of goals for our personal voyage. Along with this realistic appreciation of what is possible, given our personalities, goes an emphasis on daily coping strategies rather than on a major reconstruction of ourselves. Thus, even in the best of therapies there will be a distinct limit to what can be achieved. Having an appropriate set of expectations and goals is part of adaptive coping, and is the main thrust of this book.

# *The context around us: why do places and people matter?*

So far I have been trying to draw out the important ways in which our temperament and personality provide a personal context for the mid-life crisis. For instance, they will colour how we see this event and our reaction to a crisis – perhaps regarding it as an opportunity for growth and a chance to draw on our resilience. This personal aspect now needs to be considered in its social context. We are 'actors' on a 'stage', after all. To continue the theatrical parallel, the persona or character that you perform within life's play only makes sense in its physical and social setting. This in theatrical terms consists of the other characters within the play and the storyline or script you are all to enact. In terms of the mid-life crisis, this helpful parallel draws out two important issues: namely, the kind of social support that surrounds us; and the developmental tasks or social obligations and pressures that we feel we must address.

### *We need a place to be ourselves*

The physical context or environment may include a range of important factors, such as the space that we have available physically (such as the house we live in), and our proximity to other resources (especially social support). It also includes the social environment, which has a profound influence on how we cope. Important aspects of the social world in which we live include things like the roles that we play, the power or status that these give us, and the social support that we give and take in our daily exchanges with the significant others in our lives.

One of our 'case studies' in this book is Mike. This is a quote from one of our conversations, and it illustrates nicely this relationship between the person, the situation and life's tasks:

> *The idea of emigrating was a thrilling thought, but also a daunting one. To take my life forward in a totally new yet seemingly safe country held enormous appeal. It seemed like that place could afford me the opportunity to move on to a lifestyle that would be far more satisfying. It seemed as if I was reaching a stage in my life where high status and the day-to-day pressure and competitiveness were of less and less appeal. The option that*

*seemed to be offered to me was to move on to a new phase in my life, made possible by this brand-new environment, and especially by some particularly important people that would be part of that new life. It was like a fresh start, at a time when the familiar grind of life had become tiresome. It was an opportunity to move on to a new phase whereby I could achieve some other important goals and achieve greater satisfaction with my life.*

On the 'stage of life' our social situation is of huge importance. Without the support of others, we would not only struggle to cope with the various demands of life, we would also struggle to find any meaning to our life. After all, it is from our past and present social life that we gain a sense of what really matters. For example, our parents may convey to us the importance of achievement in our careers or of stability in our married lives. We carry this with us into our own adulthood, reflecting a socially defined value. And if something happens that interferes with our achievement or stability, then we may feel particularly uncomfortable. In such a situation, the availability of others to provide us with support is vital. This social support will interact with the physical context, because places exert a strong influence on our opportunities for social interaction. We all know, for instance, that some particular club, pub or café is good for obtaining social support, just as others are of limited help. And in turn our personalities and the tasks that we are undertaking at a particular time will interact with the situation to influence the 'give and take' of social support. Again, the comparison with the theatre is quite clear, in the sense that any actor cannot meaningfully play his or her part in the absence of other actors, an audience, a story or a stage. But when these different factors come together in the correct combination, the actor will produce his or her best performance.

A large amount of research shows that social support helps people to adapt and make good life transitions. The right physical environment for social support is also important. In one study, conducted in Norway, researchers looked at the effects on social support and the well-being of the residents that followed from changes to a local neighbourhood. The introduction of a new shopping area, complete with cinema, restaurants, a new sports arena and a primary school, was found to be associated with much improved social interaction and mental health for the residents. This

17

is similar to the role of the audience for a group of actors: the play only makes sense when there is an audience present, and the audience can, like a community, create an important context or setting for the adjustments that are enacted within the play.

## We all need the support of others

So how does what we know about social support help us to manage a mid-life crisis? In essence, it tells us that social support is essential to manage the transition successfully, and we need to make as much use as possible of the different forms of social support. These include informational, practical, emotional and companionship support.

By informational support I refer to how individuals may share useful facts or experiences. They pass on useful tips, including how different efforts at dealing with transitions worked out. This book is actually a form of informational support, as is information to be found in 'agony aunt' columns and on the internet. Obviously, information is also communicated in social settings (a good example is in religious gatherings) and among friends.

Practical support, by comparison, is built on the exchange of materials or in the supply of practical assistance. Being able to go round to a neighbour's house to borrow a tool would be an example of this. Engaging the help of a friend in addressing an aspect of the mid-life transition (e.g. help in writing letters) would be another example.

Emotional support concerns contacts with people that help us to be more aware of how we are feeling about the transition, and helps us to express feelings (such as sharing our depression). Most importantly, it can also serve to have those feelings heard and validated by someone else. In essence, we feel better about ourselves after this kind of social exchange.

Finally, companionship is a more general form of support, which is all about being accepted – of feeling like you are a part of the human race. By contrast, one of the most hurtful experiences any of us can have is to feel disconnected, rejected and isolated from others. Therefore, in tackling a mid-life crisis and in trying to make a successful transition, one would be well advised to make as much use as possible of all these four types of support. More will be said about this in Chapter 6.

So what benefits are there to be had from these different forms of social support? The answer is that engaging in informational, practical, emotional and companionship support should lead to a number of important consequences. These were hinted at above, and include a sense of 'attachment' to others, which is particularly important in allowing us to feel safe, supported, assisted and valued. A second major result of good social support is a sense of belonging and integration with others. A third outcome is feeling socially validated or recognized as a unique individual, and in terms of your general competence as a person. Lastly, good social support will guide you through the mid-life crisis, perhaps through the provision of useful advice or information.

The following quote from my talks with Teena illustrates some of these forms and functions of social support:

*Because I come from a very supportive and loving family, I knew they were there for me. When we moved away from all my social 'anchors' and things went badly wrong, I just cracked up. They all wanted to come up to help me. I felt adrift. I asked them to give me a week to get sorted out [Teena was leaving her partner and moving into a new flat] and it was terrible – I just had to get through one day at a time. But it felt as if my mum was there for me, and every day she or my sister would ring. My brothers wanted to come up too, but they were asked not to at this stage. My mum told me, though, that they sent all their love. The fact that they were there was just huge. At the time I had lots of guilt, blaming myself. Yet when I talked to my mother, I got it into context – someone else's perspective, which helped me to see how adrift my perception was. Also, my sister just allowed me to talk about how scared and confused I felt, and gave me huge support. There was no blame at all. Later they did come up and did practical things, like taking my daughter to school. I remember looking up at the year planner and saying to Mum: 'How am I going to do it?' and she just said 'You'll do it – we're here.' That was massive, and I didn't feel adrift.*

# What are the phases and tasks of life?

Most of us would sign up to Shakespeare's view that our lives consist of a number of relatively clear-cut stages. Researchers and clinicians agree on this point, though the number of phases and their basis is not yet settled. The basic idea is that we develop as we go through life. The potential for personal change and growth continues throughout our lives, but the ways in which we develop do not follow any fixed route or pattern. Another widely accepted idea is that our development occurs on a number of different fronts – say, in terms of both our work and our relationship with our partner. Lastly, the developing individual and the changing environment influence one another.

Within this general process of development there tend to be a number of phases or stages. This is partly because development is not a steady, continuous process. Rather, it follows a more fluctuating course, like the incoming tide or the changing seasons. An example would be the physical changes that unfold in our bodies naturally over time, as in the menopause. A second reason for the phases is that our environment tends to pressure us into changing at certain times, as in being of an age to start school or work. These major life events will in turn force us to develop more quickly than usual. Being more noticeable than the normal pace of development, we then tend to label such periods as particular phases.

## Eight important stages in life

One of the most famous of these accounts of life phases was provided in 1950 by Erik Erikson (see Further reading). He put forward the view that life consisted of eight stages:

1 Infancy (0–1 years)
2 Early childhood (1–6 years)
3 Play age (6–10 years)
4 School age (10–14 years)
5 Adolescence (14–20 years)
6 Young adulthood (20–35 years)
7 Maturity (35–65 years)
8 Old age (65+ years)

Erikson believed that each of these stages was related to a particular life crisis. For example, in the maturity stage of life there is a crisis over our ability to make a contribution to the lives of others and to society more generally (called *generativity*). It is based on a value of caring about the welfare of others, of establishing and guiding the next generation, and also of wishing to make one's mark, of leaving something behind that has some worth. Writing a book, painting a picture, educating others and carrying out research would all be cases in point. Being a parent, however, is probably the most common way that we can satisfy the need for generativity.

A failure to achieve this generativity was thought by Erikson to lead to individuals turning inwards and becoming self-centred. The focus then becomes their own welfare and development, often associated, he thought, with chronic illness. There may also be a significant sense of being thwarted or unfulfilled, sometimes manifesting itself in disappointment or even self-disgust or reproach, and a growing rigidity to life (e.g. working to maintain what one's life stands for, rather than encouraging others to make improvements to it; this has been referred to as 'passing on the torch').

Similar accounts of life's stages have been provided by many others, Shakespeare included. One such writer was Daniel Levinson, who in fact coined the phrase 'mid-life crisis'. He asserted that, around the age of 40, most men (his study sample) go through a phase of personal struggle, questioning much of their life and feeling that they cannot go on as before. A new path and purpose in life is what is needed, and by following this path we can develop and become more contented people (men and women alike). In this sense, 'life begins at 40'. Levinson even argued, based on his careful study of these 40 men, that those who do not question their lives or search for a new path only postpone things, and so create the basis for a later developmental crisis or simply 'withering away' (stagnating personally).

## Five tasks in life

In thinking about life in this way, we can see how certain predictable tasks may need to be tackled. The adolescents who go off to university have to grapple with numerous tasks, such as making new friends and getting their bearings in a new place. For the mid-life individual there are other challenges, as in adjusting to losses. These relate to the loss of senior family members, but also to the losses

21

associated with the ageing process, such as a woman's loss of fertility with the menopause. Again, researchers have set about labelling such characteristic tasks. Coping with a major life crisis, such as the mid-life one, is thought to entail five fundamental tasks:

1 Establishing the meaning or personal significance of the situation – after the shock and confusion, there is a need to find sense or value in the crisis.
2 Confronting reality and dealing with what needs to be tackled – which may take the form of finding a new job or building a new relationship.
3 Maintaining social supports – keeping good communication going helps the coping effort, as touched on earlier.
4 Keeping an emotional balance – upsetting feelings need to be managed well enough to allow those relationships to occur successfully and for understandable fears to be overcome.
5 Sustaining a sense of control – we need to try to keep a reasonable self-image going, and have enough confidence to go through with what needs to be done.

## Summary

In this chapter I have tried to outline why we might be experiencing the mid-life crisis at this particular point in time and have suggested that a major part of the answer is to be found by understanding the context in which the crisis arises. This context is made up of many factors, and I have emphasized the ones that have the strongest bearing on how we make the transition. This includes the physical environment, because this creates the platform or stage, influencing at times quite strongly how we interact with others and struggle or manage to cope with situations. In addition, there is a social dimension to the context, and I have suggested this is crucially important to our transition and to our general well-being. In turn, both our physical and our social worlds will interact with our personality. A further factor is the phases of adjustment that we are in while working through our transition, and the tasks that life will tend to be presenting to us at this point in time. To return to the drama parallel, while the physical environment is represented by the stage and the various arrangements on the stage, the social dimension is represented by the actors and the audience. In turn we can think of the life tasks that we face at the mid-life stage as being like the script of the play, full of challenges and problems for us to address. Out of this we try to define a path, a personally important 'plot' or 'story'.

In the next chapter I will go on to define precisely what I mean by the mid-life crisis, and then try to set out how it is different from the other transitions that we will already have gone through (e.g. those during adolescence).

## Points to Ponder

You may want to try to apply some of this material to yourself. A few key questions will probably help to focus your reflections:

- Which early childhood influences shaped your personality?
- How would you describe your personality?
- Can you recognize any lifetraps in yourself?
- How do others provide you with social support?
- How does it help you?

# 2
# Crisis

It was the best of times, and it was the worst of times.
(Charles Dickens, on the French revolution)

We all have to deal with a series of transitions during our lives. Most of these transitions will be unavoidable, and will probably take place fairly smoothly. However, there are times when the passage from one life situation to another is hazardous and creates considerable emotional distress. As we have seen in Chapter 1, this can involve particularly difficult stressors, or we may need to deal with some awkward conflicts over what to prioritize in life. The 'mid-life crisis' is a case in point, although I should make it clear that this phase is more of a popular image than a scientific 'fact'. In scientific circles, the crisis is not sufficiently clear-cut to convince researchers that it exists. Instead, they tend to view this term as a way of understanding several related physical changes and the often associated social changes.

There *is* agreement, though, that this under-researched period involves a transition, one that typically needs to be made at around the age of 40 to 50. It is a transition into middle adulthood, one that affects each one of us differently, and may be most pronounced in men. It is not an *inevitable* period of significant change for everyone, but for a considerable number of people it does mean a tumultuous struggle within the self, and with those who are close to us. For instance, some research indicates that during this period men tend to become more nurturing, while their partners become more assertive. As a result, for many it is a time of moderate to severe personal and inter-personal crisis. In this sense, the mid-life transition is one of a fairly inevitable series of changes with which we have to grapple – and one that will be a crisis for many. It is widely recognized therefore that the mid-life crisis is 'normal', but is none the less an exceptionally testing passage in one's life.

In this chapter we will consider some of the challenges that this particular transition includes, and then discuss in detail some of the special reasons for this crisis. Emphasis will be given to the positive aspects, alongside the more familiar difficulties that the crisis throws up. Finally, we will end the chapter with some suggestions for making sense of the crisis – a vital part of successful coping.

## What are the ingredients for a crisis?

The mid-life period has usually been viewed as a time when we are at the height of our powers, including having the best jobs and general quality of life that we will ever enjoy. But, strangely enough, this is also the time of the mid-life crisis. Why should this seeming paradox occur? Perhaps it is because this is also a period in which we typically have to deal with such issues as children becoming teenagers or leaving home, ageing or dying parents who need our care, career options becoming limited, the variety or power in our working life decreasing, physical decline, and a general decrease in the extent to which we seem to occupy centre-stage at important events (e.g. at weddings, promotions at work, or births of children). Others describe discontent and restiveness, or a sense of being 'expendable'. As a result of these and other changes, the mid-life stage will often entail some tricky and possibly competing responsibilities, such as managing challenging adolescents while also serving as a carer for one of our parents. These responsibilities tend to arise at a time when our dependence on others for support tends to decrease, and our physical capabilities may become more limited. For the first time maybe, we have to accept the weakening of the flesh, the loss of our fitness and energy. A quote from Mike seems to bear this out:

> *Having been super-fit all my life, it was a real shock to realize how my body was definitely winding down. For years I'd felt the need to push my body to its limit, and had enjoyed the ability to stride up hills, cycle all day long, or toil in the garden. Gradually it dawned on me that my muscles were shrinking and the old energy was lacking. My body shape also started to change, with a double chin, a bulging belly and a general sagging down.*

Of course, Mike – or anyone else – may well have had somewhat similar experiences in the past (following a period of illness, for example), but what is strikingly different this time is the unmistakable hand of Father Time behind these unwelcome changes. From a psychological point of view this is a critical difference, as it means recognizing a loss of control over events – and ones that matter deeply. This stage may, then, be viewed as a transition from being in control of one's destiny to having to hand over control to the inevitable forces of time and nature. That this should happen at the height of one's powers in one respect (e.g. financial etc.) is particularly difficult to accept – and indeed, many will struggle heroically to halt the tide of time: working out twice as hard, eating more carefully than ever, or investing in expensive beauty products. But while we double our efforts, we get half the return – things are beginning to go against us, and there seems to be nothing we can do to win this struggle against time!

Here we have two potent ingredients for a crisis – a loss of control over the ageing process, and a loss of power to remedy matters. Additionally, this is a new and deeply worrying realization, as previously we had always had control or at least some power – in other words, time was basically on our side. If things are now more difficult to rectify or influence, then we are entering uncharted, deeply worrying waters (e.g. the menopause in women or changes in body shape for men).

Therefore, perhaps the single most important cause of the mid-life crisis is that of coming to terms with how the rest of our life is going to be, and this realization has to draw on how things have been for us in the past. In this sense, the mid-life crisis normally pivots on a reassessment of what has gone before and what lies ahead. Characteristic questions include: 'Have I done the right thing with my life?', 'Is there time to change?', 'What are the things I would like to achieve in the second half of my life?' Many researchers and clinicians would say that driving this reassessment of our life is our first frightening glimpse of our mortality, and this may lead into a fundamental review of such things as our marriage, personal priorities, and even our most basic values.

## So what is the 'mid-life crisis'?

To begin with, the term 'crisis' is much maligned. According to dictionary definitions, 'crisis' is defined as a moment of danger or suspense that facilitates decision-making and enables a turning point to occur. This point is important to stress, in line with the positive tone of this book. The word 'crisis' comes from the Greek *krinein*, which literally means 'to decide'. The term 'mid-life crisis', therefore, pivots around the idea that it is *a time at which especially important decisions need to be made*, because time is thought to be running out. Following this logic, we can again think of the mid-life crisis in terms of a long sea journey, during which a big decision needs to be made, in terms of correcting one's course. The decision to change direction would come from this reassessment, especially in deciding the most important 'destinations' in what remains of one's life or journey.

The mid-life crisis is unlike many other life transitions or crises because it centres so fundamentally on the realization of our past disappointments and failures. The physical changes that inevitably take place as one reaches mid-life are an undeniable pointer to our approaching death, or in the nearer future to our physical decline – and with this the possible dependence upon others. Part of the problem is that this physical decline, unlike most early transitions, represents an important change that cannot ultimately be controlled or reversed. Arising out of the reassessment of one's life thus far, there may also be a realization that many of one's childhood ideals have not been – and now cannot be – achieved. This may include career expectations or a belief in one's ability to succeed in other areas of life, such as in sport or in acquiring material wealth. A sense of being 'thwarted' can therefore emerge, contributing to feeling angry or depressed (this point will be continued in Chapter 6).

On the positive side, a distinctive priority for the future usually becomes the need to contribute to the lives of others, and of accepting one's social responsibilities. There can be a keen sense that, whatever the drawbacks and limitations that ageing brings, time is now precious and there is important work to be done. As Mike says in the quote on page 32, 'life is too short' for living lies or for frittering time away.

This sense of well-judged direction and subjective urgency is perhaps the third defining feature of the mid-life crisis: there is somewhere we need to go, and we are determined to get there.

# What causes a mid-life crisis?

### A 'breaking point'

At one level, it is fairly obvious what causes the mid-life crisis: if one is confronted with a powerful mixture of demands at a time when one is particularly sensitive about one's own functioning, then crisis is the obvious result. And, as noted in the previous chapter, there are some particularly demanding tasks to be dealt with during the mid-life period. The existence of these tasks, though, does not fully explain the emergence of a *crisis*. This brings us back to the point that some people handle such stressors more readily than others. Also, each of us will vary in terms of how well we manage different demands at different times. This can depend on such general things as how we are succeeding in related areas, such as at work or in our relationships.

This explanation for the mid-life crisis might be thought of as a *breaking point*, when a crisis occurs because there is sufficient pressure to cause us to reach a turning point in our life. This is the point when we recognize that major changes simply *must* occur in order for things to improve. It is a point of near desperation, where something simply has to give (i.e. things need to change). An example might be being made redundant and acknowledging that our past career is no longer a viable option. We might then introduce a major change of direction, by retraining for a more promising career. Perhaps a more common example of this crisis point is divorce, as illustrated by part of Teena's tale:

> *I knew I just couldn't go on – what was happening was unacceptable. You just get to the point where you've tried everything and there's nothing left to try. I knew at midnight one night that there was no going back. I just thought, 'no more'. I'd got to the end, the bottom. I stayed awake all night planning my move and the next day I just moved out – I had to get out.*

### A 'crystallization of all one's discontents'

A second cause of a mid-life crisis can, strangely, be the *absence* of any major demands on a person. In other words, it can arise from the realization that there are several nagging concerns that have perhaps

29

been bubbling away below our full awareness for some time, which then finally reach a point that requires change. One way of thinking about this is that of changing our daily habits. Whether it is the way we use alcohol or commit ourselves to work, habitual patterns of coping with life may gradually become unacceptable. This may happen now, even though we have been aware of some unhappiness about the habit for many years. Something, however, causes this dissatisfaction to reach crisis point, where we feel that decisions about improved habits are now needed. For example, the gap between how we are and how we ought to be may be brought to our attention by a friend or a critic. For instance, somebody may point once more to a bad habit, and for some reason on this particular occasion this comment will tip the balance and lead us to review the way we have been living this particular part of our life. This process can lead to surprisingly abrupt and major changes, worthy of the title 'mid-life crisis'. Or they can be just as important in creating the need for a fresh direction, a new way of seeing or being.

Some have referred to this relatively undramatic cause of the mid-life crisis as the *crystallization of all one's discontents*. In this process of crystallization, our multiple but minor complaints, misgivings or faulty habits may be brought together by some equally minor event. Perhaps because this minor event occurs when it does, during the period of significant life review, for the first time it brings all these other minor matters together. A classic example of this relatively minor trigger would be a marital conflict that may have occurred many times previously, but which during a critical part of the mid-life crisis touches a raw nerve. An example from John's experience was his inflexible wife:

> *For years we'd got by, even though I'd always found her stubborn side a real trial. Somehow we'd make light of it and keep things going OK. But it bothered me that I was the one who was always expected to smooth things over, to give in and sort of accept the blame. Then when something else went wrong, this long-simmering aggravation tipped the balance and made me stop and do some hard thinking.*

Another general example of the mid-life period is a conflict between 'achievement' (as in seeking to obtain the best possible jobs or the greatest possible material wealth) and *affiliation* (i.e. a sense of belonging and giving to our nearest and dearest, as well as to society more generally). This conflict between achievement and affiliation may reach a head and so cause a mid-life crisis. We may be forced to deal with the well-worn question 'Who am I?' Although perhaps posed many times previously, the question may, at the point of a conflict, trigger a significant decision, such as to do 'what matters'.

## A 'transforming experience'

A third possible cause of a crisis is having a powerful, positive experience that is so important that it transforms our life. An illustration would be a near-death experience. In this explanation, people who have gone through a mid-life crisis look back on this major experience as the turning point, the time when they knew that a new phase of their life was beginning; this experience is often described as being quite different from any relevant prior experiences. At the very least it accelerates the normal process of transition during mid-life, but more often it is described as dramatically changing our direction. What seems to be particularly important about this experience is that it marks a maturation or new stage of development for the individual. The experience provides something that moves us on, with a sense of gratitude for the development. We can therefore call this third cause the *transforming experience*.

A particularly dramatic example of the 'transforming experience' behind the mid-life crisis is the so-called psychological 'epiphany'. This experience occurs suddenly, leading to a profound, positive and lasting change in the way we think about ourselves and the world. The following quote from Mike illustrates this sort of experience:

> *I had received an exciting invitation to travel to Canada on a prestigious visit. For reasons that were not clear to me at the time, my partner was reluctant to accompany me. Because I had long wished to explore Canada, I took two weeks of leave to supplement the business side of the trip. During this time I travelled by car throughout this stunningly beautiful country and I travelled alone. The country was strangely reminiscent of home, but more characteristic of how home would have been in my childhood. This combination of a strangely familiar, stunningly beautiful country and the temporary experience of being alone*

*after many years of married life had a profound effect on my perspective on life. I was aware that my perspective was different, though it seemed to happen automatically. Quite suddenly and with exceptional clarity I came to the view that life was too short for living a lie in my life. I kept thinking 'life is too short'. As a result, I formed the unshakeable conviction that my marriage, which had been rocky for some years, should now be brought to an end. What's more, the ending should be one that was handled with great sensitivity and compassion, in terms of the lengthy discussions that would be necessary with my partner. To my great relief, when I summarized this experience and declared my belief that life was too short to go on with what had become a pointless marriage, my partner totally agreed and even congratulated me on having the courage to make a decision on the matter!*

This quote contains several of the explanations for the crisis touched on above, but in particular it contains some of the features of the 'epiphany' experience. That is, there was a sense that something very clear and vivid had happened, something quite extraordinary, that had led the individual concerned to think that life would never be quite the same again. Second, there was an element of surprise – a sudden discovery of how things might be different. This is unlike normal decision-making, which tends to be gradual, with deliberate efforts to change our minds. Mike's epiphany wasn't something that he *did*; rather, it was something that just happened to him. There was a strong quality of 'newness', of feeling that there had been a special experience. A third feature of the epiphany is that what has been experienced is viewed as positive and beneficial. Finally, there is a sense of permanence to the decisions that are made during the epiphany experience – a sense of there being 'no turning back'. One is changed for ever, and aware that the only possible next step is onward from the fundamental insight that one has gained.

### 'Special kinds of people'

A fourth way of understanding the cause of the mid-life crisis is to think about it as something that only happens to certain kinds of people. In this sense, the crisis indicates a special kind of individual, perhaps someone whose life experiences or outlook lend them to a positive-change experience.

There is, in fact, a long history to this supposed cause. In the past, the emotional sensitivity, suggestibility and sense that one's experiences arise from unknown sources have been considered bases for the mid-life crisis. Such characteristics have been thought to account for sudden impulses to act in certain ways and the somewhat spontaneous writing of literature, apparently appearing out of nowhere. These *special kinds of people* are credited with typically having a more intuitive grasp of life or a 'sixth sense'. Connected to this way of thinking is a tendency to understand things quite suddenly, instead of as a result of a gradual, logical process. These people tend to have insights and to suddenly 'get it'. Some people even recount mystical experiences, something that also has a very long history. This type of experience is typically difficult to express to others, and may also make us quite uneasy, as such occurrences challenge our normal beliefs. However, it is common for people who have had a mystical experience to view the logical, material world in a much more definite perspective, as something that is only a small part of a much greater and more important reality. A consequence tends to be devotion to compassionate service for others and a partial rejection of materialism. This is a good example of one of the fundamental changes that can occur, this time to our value system. In such a position, individuals may regard the crisis very positively. They may say that without it they wouldn't have achieved what they now regard as a better approach to life. In effect, a crisis leads to important decisions that have improved the quality of their lives.

## A spiritual encounter

The fifth popular explanation for a mid-life crisis is a sense of being in the presence of some holy or spiritual being. Many of those who have been interviewed about the onset of their crisis report insights arising from the 'presence of God', or some similar sacred encounter.

This kind of explanation also has a long history, and various traditions have held on to the belief that people can tap into a spiritual dimension. In Buddhism, for example, we might (through meditation and other exercises) come to experience a sacred 'oneness' with nature. There is a kind of breakthrough in our awareness of the way the world is, which leads to a redirecting of our energies in life. There is indeed reason to believe that we may be

to a spiritual experience because of certain states that we
olonged physical or emotional distress, leading to a point of
ᴜᴄ, tion, is an illustration. Conversely, others believe that some
divine force or god has singled them out for the blessing that
emerges from their mid-life crisis.

### Some or all of the above

Of course, the above explanations may occur in different combinations. Equally, given our limited scientific understanding of such
dramatic change, there may be some totally fresh explanation, one
that provides a much better understanding. Indeed, as in the spiritual
explanation, perhaps it is because of our limited understanding that
we tend to construe change in supernatural or mysterious ways.

### My preferred explanation for a mid-life crisis

Since this book draws on good scientific evidence wherever possible,
I prefer the most convincing explanation for the mid-life crisis.
According to this view, a mid-life crisis is a special kind of transition
that is triggered by a major event or stressor. This is the crisis that
creates a need for a significant life review, and a major decision to
change the way that we live. There is often a strong sense of disquiet
or unhappiness with the way things have become, and an equally
powerful need to determine a new and better way to live the
remainder of our life; and this calls upon our personal coping
strategies and our social supporters (especially family and friends) if
we are to make the transition successfully. Because they are so
central, it is to these coping strategies that a major chunk of this
book is dedicated; it is the way that we adapt on life's stage that is so
crucial. Second, concentrating on coping suggests what we might be
able to do to make a successful transition. For this reason, the next
three chapters address different ways of coping with the crisis.

## There is good news!

Although many of those experiencing a mid-life crisis may (at least
initially) also experience unhappiness or mild depression, the
majority of those who have gone through with the transition report
positive benefits. These people will tend to experience the mid-life

crisis as an opportunity for growth or positive change, and see it as a time to focus on the things in life that they feel are important – a time for withdrawal from wasteful, energy-consuming activities that lack true satisfaction. Teena's tale again reflects this personal growth:

> *While I regretted the break-up of my marriage, and hated being alone, as I came through it I began to get stronger, more determined. I thought 'I can do this', and it'll be worth it. I realized that things can go wrong, but I can still build a life, learning and feeling stronger. I became less fearful, harder, and better able to cope. I was more protective of myself, and more independent: I realized I could exist outside the marriage.*

Post mid-life crisis, people have also been found to have decreased their dependence on others, reduced their self-criticism, while at the same time increasing their confidence and decisiveness. Because they are comfortable about their newly defined personal values and their life purpose, they may also feel more content with their life circumstances.

## *Summary*

In this chapter I have suggested that our life is actually made up of a series of transitions, which are brought about by a variety of factors. These factors include changes to our physical self (e.g. the surge of adolescence or the arrival of the menopause) and related changes in other important spheres of our life (e.g. in relationships and at work). These transitions incorporate a number of challenges or tasks which, if handled successfully, move us in a positive way to new periods of relative stability and comfort. In time, however, this will lead to another period of significant transition. It follows that our task is to understand and cope with the sure-fire need to make transitions if we are to succeed in our personal 'struggle for existence'. Also, we need to see the challenge as positively as possible. In particular, the mid-life crisis may best be thought of as an opportunity for particularly important growth or development, towards achieving our potential. If we see the difficulties in such a positive light, we are well on the way to coping with the crisis successfully. Indeed, one of the major messages of the mid-life crisis is a positive one (e.g. the experience of 'epiphany'). This remarkable experience, which seems to be reported by quite a large proportion of those who had a significant mid-life crisis, is one that leaves the individual who has experienced it profoundly and positively transformed.

In conclusion, the mid-life crisis can be a healthy transition, given that it is a time of so many significant changes. It creates the need to review one's life. The time that has passed up until this mid-life point is often filled with regrets and disappointments, but the time that is left for us to live needs to be organized so that life is not too short for us to achieve what has come to matter most to us.

## Points to Ponder

- How can you make sense of your own transitions?
- Do you recognize any of the above causes of mid-life crises in your own experience of change (e.g. a 'breaking point')?
- What would you say was special or different about the mid-life transition?

# 3

## Construing: making sense of your experience

It is not events that disturb people but rather the view that they take of those events.

(Ecclesiastes)

In the previous chapter I tried to draw attention to the powerful influence that the context can have on our crisis. At least two important aspects of the context were highlighted: the physical 'stage' on which we act out our crisis; and the personal history that relates to the situation – particularly as it is built into our personality. In this chapter, I will go on to show how these contextual factors are brought together through the ways in which we try to understand or make sense of our situation.

This effort at appraising our situation will be referred to as 'construing'. The word is a good one, as it comes from the Latin word that means 'construction'. This is appropriate because, as indicated by the quote from Ecclesiastes above, it is important to realize that events do not simply occur to us as if they were fixed and objective facts. Rather, we *make something* of events: building a sensible, subjective construction out of what is happening to us. Construing is where the different things happening around and inside us are made into something that has personal meaning. It is the point at which we can start to make sense of the things that are going on, and to interpret a situation in relation to ourselves. It is the sort of attitude or stance that we adopt on life's stage as we play out our part.

I will next outline how this stance helps us to construct a meaningful experience of the world, and then go on to consider a number of different ways in which we normally construe events. These different ways have a vital influence on how we decide to deal with situations, and in turn with how we feel and function. Again, some illustrative 'personal story' material from Teena, Mike and John will be used to illustrate these points.

## *Does it matter how we construe things?*

Normally, life is an unending series of stressful events – but, contrary to popular opinion, such stress is vital for our well-being and happiness. Indeed, one of the surest ways to drive a person mad is to *remove* all forms of stress. For instance, the 'sensory deprivation' – a deliberate removal of stress – that can arise in solitary confinement during imprisonment is likely to provoke hallucinations. Stress is the basis on which healthy and valued change occurs, and the foundation on which we as individuals develop. But beyond their stimulus role, the stressors themselves are of little importance. One person's major life event is another person's routine 'day in the life'. So, while you or I may find moving house or changing jobs very taxing, the next person will be quite excited and enthusiastic about such stressors.

Stress, then, can be understood partly on the basis of how our personalities differ. But there is also a general, shared sense in which stressful events are construed and can be perceived as more or less challenging for us all. As we shall see, what makes us have a common reaction to events is the shared meaning that the events can have for us all. For example, if a stressful event signals that we will be socially isolated or rejected, then that will be an unpleasant experience for most of us. However, we do not all see particular events as carrying the same underlying threat. Indeed, each of us may respond differently over time to the same stressful event. At one point in time a friend's rather cool refusal of a social invitation may cause significant distress because it signals rejection. A few weeks later, perhaps because we are in a different frame of mind, the same event will not cause any distress whatsoever. Therefore, we have to have a way of understanding how it is that events are understood, and how this understanding gives them meaning, which then shapes our reactions so profoundly, yet flexibly.

As Brown and Harris put it, 'everything turns on the meaningfulness of events' (Brown and Harris, 1978). As we noted earlier, these researchers looked at the process by which people became depressed, and they found that stress or change in itself was of no importance. What seemed to matter was the sense that these individuals made of their circumstances. The stressors or crises that Brown and Harris took into account included being made redundant, a major material loss or general disappointment, a life-threatening illness occurring in a close relative, or the actual separation from a key figure in one's life. Not only did Brown and Harris emphasize how everything turned on the way that people construed these stressful events, they also clarified that when this construction indicated that the event was only a short-term threat, it did not lead to the onset of depression. It was only when the events were construed as long-term threats (and where there was also some weakness or vulnerability in the individual's ability to manage the stressor) that they found people reporting depression. The research showed that ongoing major difficulties, such as poor health or relationship struggles, were another important influence on the occurrence of depression. They then concluded that while major life events can be seen as *provoking agents*, these are rarely sufficient to bring about depression. Also involved were so-called *vulnerability factors* – such as the lack of a close confiding relationship with another person (such as a partner or family member). (We will return to the importance of such social support in Chapters 5 and 6.) Other social factors, such as unemployment or lack of money, will also contribute to depression (we saw how such contextual factors were important in the previous chapter). But the *most* important factor, according to Brown and Harris, was whether these events and circumstances carried *meaningful implications* for the individual – in other words, there was usually something in particular that 'brought home' the importance of the events and circumstances. Therefore how we construe things matters hugely, in terms of how stress makes us feel, and in terms of who we are. What lies at the heart of the meaning or construction we form of events is usually close to the core of our personality – namely, our sense of self, our identity.

## What is the right attitude to have towards events in our lives?

So it seems clear that the way we look at events in order to make sense of our situation is crucial. This is an important point, because it means we are not helpless in the face of stress. Also, it makes it possible for us to influence how we respond to and come to feel about those same events. If, for example, we think of a particularly difficult period as a 'transition' or a 'challenge' (i.e. as a natural period of change that involves difficulties that we can probably manage), then we are likely to feel energized and capable of responding. There is a 'can do' attitude to the situation. Or, to put it another way, the glass is half full, not half empty. This perspective might include seeing a mid-life crisis as an important turning point, a period to change from an unsatisfactory state of affairs to a more pleasing one. When adopting this attitude, middle age is not viewed as a crisis in a negative sense: rather, it is a long-overdue opportunity to make some important changes. Some people have thought of this period of life as a 'mid-course correction', something that allows us to steer a better course through the next phase of our life. This may involve us changing our jobs, or at least the way in which we approach our work. One example is the shift from emphasizing achievement (i.e. in competing strenuously to win the different 'badges' of success in our field) to a stance in which 'affiliation' is given priority. In using this term I mean the greater value we might decide to give to friends and relationships, or to other things that may now seem more important in life. The following quote is from Mike, and it illustrates just such a positive attitude towards what might otherwise have been seen as a life-shattering event at work – redundancy:

*Someone asked me whether I had any regrets. On the one hand I definitely had, which was that it had happened at all. It wasn't something that one would wish for. I also regretted that I hadn't tried harder to make things work out. It would have been better to have hung in and work towards some kind of better outcome. On the other hand, I have absolutely no regrets. I thought then (now over two years ago), and I think just as definitely now, that it was probably for the best. It was tough, but it was right under the circumstances. It happened at a time when our children had left home to go about the world in their own independent ways. This meant there was less risk or responsibility connected with being a worker, and more time to give to my own interests. This was a time of thinking about the benefits and pleasures that life could bring. Staying in a pointless job was obviously something that had to stop if this better quality of life was to begin.*

*Importantly, I reckoned I was strong enough and able enough*

*to manage what would undoubtedly be a very trying time. I could
see that even though the tunnel might be dark and uncomfortable,
the light at the end of it would make it worthwhile. I decided quite
consciously to focus on what mattered most and to ending things
that got in the way.*

## How do we construe events?

What Mike tells us is that important events in life can be seen in a
different light. Just as the people interviewed in the Brown and
Harris research (Brown and Harris, 1978) were found to experience
depression depending on how they viewed things, so Mike was able
to cope better with a major life transition – that of unemployment –
by adopting a positive attitude towards events.

I am now going to say a bit more about this process of thinking
about events in a way that turns out to be helpful to our own
transition. The first basic point is that this way of looking at things is
part of how we *cope*. This is not meant in a negative sense, as in
managing somehow to get by in life. Rather, I mean the way in
which we manage to overcome the difficulties that we come across
in life. Coping is a process of adjustment, made up of how we think,
feel or act in order to try and manage stressful events.

There are two stages to our construing. The first stage happens
very quickly and perhaps even without us realizing it, and it leads us
to judge whether something affects us directly. It is an appraisal
about whether we have a stake, interest or concern in the unfolding
event, and whether it is likely that we will have an emotional
reaction to it. This means that the initial construction we place on
events needs to be thought about in terms of how it is relevant to our
goals, as in being something that gets in the way of what we are
trying to do (e.g. something going wrong when we are trying to
repair something). If we appraise something as being irrelevant to
our goals, then we will give it no further attention.

A second kind of interpretation is judging whether or not
something that matters threatens to either harm us or offer some
benefit to us. Depending on this construction of events, we will
either seek ways to minimize the harm, or we will seek ways to seek
the maximum benefit from something that has arisen – for example,

if we are involved in some marital dispute and see an opportunity to talk about something in a way that helps us both to benefit from a situation.

If we go back to Mike's story, we can see some examples of this process at work in his thinking about his divorce. In terms of goals, he laid considerable stress on what really mattered most to him. This was the longer-term quality of his life, versus the pretence that he was living in a satisfactory marriage. Second, he also saw gains resulting from divorce, rather than appraising the situation as potentially harmful.

In summary, we can construe events as relevant or irrelevant, and then as potentially harmful or beneficial. Either way, such construing lies at the heart of how we react to and are affected by the things that take place during the mid-life crisis.

## What are the main ways to construe events?

Hopefully it is now becoming clear that a great deal hinges on the way that we interpret what is happening to us. Researchers have tried to list the main ways in which we tend to appraise events; these include things like whether or not a stressful event has happened to us before (novelty). In most cases, we will feel better able to cope with a stressful event with which we have dealt successfully in the past. Second, having some forewarning or even control over when a stressor occurs is likely to be helpful. In this sense, one may know for sure within a long-standing marriage, for example, that certain actions that one might take will lead to an argument, or some other predictable outcome. This tends to make the ultimate occurrence of that argument more bearable. Just as importantly, it tends to mean that our coping strategies are better placed to deal with that event, because we are not so stressed by it. The text in the box below lists these and other common ways of construing what is happening to us, but first let's look at an example in relation to Teena's story:

*I had a long-term fear of losing everything – my security, a beautiful home, my family. Then things went badly wrong. Despite my numerous attempts – I tried everything – I was unable to save my marriage. It dawned on me that I had to get out to save my self-esteem. Whatever lay ahead had to be better. I was prepared to face anything and I wouldn't be beaten. When I left I blamed myself – I tortured myself. Now I realize, some years down the line, that he did not care enough – he wasn't strong enough to deal with things. I realized he just couldn't cope.*

*Ten ways to construe or make sense of the things that happen to us. Depending on how we construe things, different reactions will follow.*

| Ways to construe the things that happen to us | Example |
| --- | --- |
| 1 'Novelty' | Not having faced a problem or event like this before |
| 2 'Predictability' | Knowing that something was going to happen – an expected event |
| 3 'Readiness' | Having enough time to prepare us to deal with the stress |
| 4 'Threat' | Seeing something as likely to hurt or harm us |
| 5 'Challenge' | Treating an event as something we can rise to and beat |
| 6 'Responsibility' | The problem being caused by something that we did |
| 7 'Blame' | The stress was caused by something someone else did |
| 8 'Benefit' | Some good will come out of the situation |
| 9 'Resolution' | The problem can be brought to an end |
| 10 'Success' | When the situation or event is brought to an end, it will work out well for us |

As the text in the box shows, in addition to the novelty or predictability of some stressful event, it is also important to have enough time to prepare for it (readiness), to tend to see something more as a challenge than a threat if at all possible, and to recognize that we have some responsibility for what has happened. To continue with the example of marital discord, driving home from work we might realize that it was likely that there would be another argument that evening. We might then use the time available while driving to get ready for this unfortunate event. But in fact just thinking of it as 'unfortunate' indicates that we are tending to see the argument as a threat rather than a challenge. We might then, as part of the immediate coping effort, convince ourselves that it is better to think of the argument as a challenge and to take responsibility for it. This is not to suggest that arguments in themselves are good or desirable, but rather that we need to try and convert an important discussion into something that is as useful as possible, and something that causes as little distress as possible.

In Teena's example, we can see that she did have some 'predictability' and 'readiness', as her situation was worsening steadily. The break-up of her marriage was seen as both a threat and an opportunity. She had to get out of what she called a 'mentally harmful situation' and get her son to a safe place where he could develop normally. She also partly blamed her husband for what was going wrong, but in time she came to construe his failure to sort things out as down to his own poor coping. She eventually came to see her own coping as ultimately being successful – it had worked out well. Teena's confidence and quality of life, and her son's growing independence, were down to her efforts.

Other important ways of construing that are listed in the box on page 43 include whether or not something that has happened was down to something that we did (blame), and whether or not something good will come out of the situation. In this way, an argument might be turned around into a discussion in which we accept at least part of the blame for something that has happened, and work hard with our partner to identify the benefits for both of us as a result of the matters we have discussed. The sort of question that can help in this situation includes asking one another what is it that would make a change worthwhile. In other words, 'In what ways might this situation be used to our advantage?' Perhaps you can see that these questions open up the possibility for moving the relationship on – even if that means divorce, if that is actually what is most beneficial, all things considered. The questions basically make it easier to see 'the wood for the trees' and allow both parties to express some genuine feelings, even if these are unwelcome sentiments. However, in my experience, I have found that the supposedly unwelcome sentiments have usually been fully antici- pated by the other party. I am struck by how often the feelings one party experiences about a situation are mirrored by the feelings that the other person experiences. Because of this, it is not a rude awakening for the other person if you reveal how you are feeling about the situation: they probably already know! Making the time and effort to express these already largely understood sentiments and views will therefore be beneficial in several ways. It can help to clear the air and shows a willingness to talk openly. It can also help to move us on to the same wavelength, creating the basis for a mutually beneficial solution to emerge: a 'win-win' approach.

This brings us on to the ninth way of construing that is listed in the box on page 43 – 'resolution'. Seeing that there might be some way of bringing things to a satisfactory end can give one strength and hope. Mike had worked carefully with his partner to try to maximize the chances that they would both achieve some favourable resolution to the difficult marital situation. Obviously, the more that different people in any situation can identify 'win-win' solutions (whether it is in terms of marriage, work, or something else), then the greater their commitment to coping with the stressor, as opposed to avoiding or escaping from it.

## *What kind of assumptions underlie these appraisals?*

There are three main assumptions we all tend to make about the world that we live in. These assumptions are things about which we are not truly conscious, but which we believe to underlie our world, and this includes the way that we construe things.

The first of these assumptions is a belief in our own invulnerabil- ity. Although at one level all of us acknowledge that one day we will die, in the meantime we actually behave as if nothing could possibly kill us. Although we recognize that it might be dangerous to cross the road without looking, we do not actually believe that we are going to get run over by a bus. We feel that such things happen to other people. This assumption that we are invulnerable is shattered, though, in such situations as serious road accidents, where people have narrowly escaped death. A common reaction that survivors of such traumas have is the realization that they were indeed close to losing their lives. This experience shatters their assumption that they were invulnerable in some way, and for many survivors this is one of the hardest things to deal with.

A second major assumption is that the world is a meaningful place and that *things make sense or have some purpose*. This is of course an attractive view and one that is strongly reinforced in our culture. Whether it is some type of religious ceremony, or simply the shared celebration of some national event (e.g. Christmas), our society gives importance to certain events – which in turn give our world a rich sense of meaning. Marriage is a case in point. It is celebrated socially as a hugely meaningful life event, primarily for the 'happy couple'. In turn, the marriage gives meaning to other people's roles, be they in-laws or children. It is also a basis on which we relate to other people, say at work, and socially it creates other meaningful situations (e.g. dinner parties or shared holidays). This quote from John's story shows how a traumatic event can upset this assumption:

*Everything seemed so straightforward and logical until my marriage fell apart. It had not been great, but it was safe and secure. Then, after 20 years, I had to think again and I had to do it from square one – all that I had thought was sacrosanct was just blown away. Everything was turned upside down. I hadn't realized just how much I'd invested in my marriage as the basis of my life. For a while nothing made any sense – it was a topsy-turvy time, and I lost my bearings.*

The third and final major assumption that we all tend to make is to see ourselves as *having a positive influence*. As in the illustration of marital arguments presented earlier, in a trivial sense it is of course common for us to tend to see our side of the argument as the correct one, and our view of the world as in some sense inherently right or preferable. More profoundly, we like to think of our life as having

46

some kind of useful purpose for others, even if we do not have an obviously 'helping' role – such as being a teacher or nurse.

## *Summary*

It is important to realize, just as the ancient Greeks did, that it is not events themselves that are stressful or upsetting, it is how we come to view those events, the meaning or sense that we ascribe to them (e.g. in their having a high threat value and no benefit). As shown in the box on page 43, these and other ways of constructing reality carry huge implications for how we cope and how we feel about events.

Because our appraisal of reality is partly a conscious process, this phase of the coping mechanism is like a critical switch, one that we can influence directly. If we develop our awareness of these ways of initially appraising events, we can come to a better realization of how our own personality shapes the way that we construe and cope. Ultimately, this influences how we feel about our lives and live them. If we construe the life events that we associate with our mid-life crisis as being uncontrollable and down to somebody else's wrong-doing, as leading to no possible benefit and over which we have absolutely no control, then we will tend to undermine our potential for adaptive coping. In turn, this will lead to a lowered quality of life. Alternatively, construing the very same stressors more positively, by thinking long and hard about how we can manage the situation and cope more successfully, we can convert the situation into an opportunity for a long-overdue transition to a better state. The key is to see the crisis as an opportunity for growth or development, rather than some dreaded signal of unstoppable decline. It is therefore vital that we construct a version of the situation that enables us to move on successfully. Whether it is the view that death is imminent or that valued roles in life are evaporating, it seems clear that the mid-life period is peculiarly stressful for many people, particularly for those who are open to and aware of events. This set of circumstances throws down a particular gauntlet: the challenge of finding meaning in our situation.

Hopefully this chapter has helped you to understand how we give meaning to our crisis and also how that process of giving meaning can be brought into focus for our benefit. In the next chapter I will go on to detail some specific ways of coping that also draw on our way of thinking about our world.

## Points to Ponder

- Can you think of recent examples where you have construed something in a way that was (a) harmful to your coping; (b) helpful to your coping?
- Have you ever had an experience that made you realize that you were assuming your invulnerability, that you felt you were a positive influence, or that the world was a meaningful place?
- Do you tend to construe things in any particular way (e.g. as 'challenging')?

# 4

# Changing behaviour: thinking your way through the crisis

Men are not prisoners of fate, but only prisoners of their own minds.

(Roosevelt)

If we are prisoners of our own minds, how can we get out of our jail? If we are already well on our way to transcending our crisis, what are we thinking that is aiding the transition? In this chapter, we will build on the message of the last chapter to suggest how we can change our fate by altering the way we think. In the last chapter, we looked at a number of different ways in which we could make sense of the things that are happening to us. As you will recall, this construing helps us to decide whether or not something requires us to respond or not, and then will help us to decide how best to respond, if that is what we need to do. This chapter concentrates on one of three fundamental ways of responding to events such as a life crisis – namely, *the way that we think about things*. (The other two ways are how we act and how we feel, and these are the focus of subsequent chapters.) As an ancient philosopher once put it, it is not events themselves that upset us, but rather the view that we take of those events. This being so, let us consider how we can improve our view.

## *How can thinking help us?*

This book is based on the belief that the ways in which we cope with our circumstances has huge significance. Coping is the way in which we respond to problems and other situations that we construe as relevant to our well-being and which we feel we have some capacity to resolve. There is a very wide range of coping strategies available to us, ones that we have learnt during our lifetime. Some of these strategies are widely accepted as being helpful or 'adaptive', while others are more commonly thought of as unhelpful or maladaptive coping strategies. For instance, trying to step back from something upsetting, in order to make some sense of the situation and to plan how best to respond to it, would be regarded as an adaptive coping strategy. Less likely to help would be thinking patterns that distract us from dealing with something problematic. For example, we have probably all heard of the term *denial*, meaning that we unconsciously avoid facing up to something that upsets us. There are of course many more such strategies than these, and indeed it is important to realize that ways of coping that are thought of as maladaptive may sometimes work well – at least in the short term. In this sense, strategies such as denial or avoidance may help us to deal with a very difficult but temporary problem for which there is no other way of coping. A crucial issue arising from this is that we should judge the effectiveness of our coping in terms of whether or not it works. In other words, the acid test of coping is how well it adapts us for our current context. Does it help us to sail life's seven seas, or does our coping make for problematic voyaging? I shall return to this point later on, as it is a vital part of our appraisal of how we cope.

### Thinking can help us to find meaning in a crisis

One of the first reactions we commonly experience when something terrible happens is to deny its existence. Things can be so overwhelming or tragic that it seems impossible that they have actually happened. It is literally unbelievable. Once we can begin to take in the event, though, we may feel waves of anger or great depths of guilt (e.g. when overtaken by something like a sudden loss). The ways that we think about such an event are likely to include disbelief, confusion, a preoccupation with the person or event that shocked us, and maybe even some odd mental experiences – like experiencing hallucinations.

Thinking can help us by creating some pattern or meaning out of such a crisis. In the case of the loss of a loved one, or indeed the loss of some ability or possession, we can begin to make sense of things by first accepting the reality of such a loss. Before we can properly adapt and make progress, though, we need to stop avoiding thinking about it and start to work on ways to address the situation or to minimize the loss. This includes taking a new perspective on things, as in emphasizing certain beliefs, or reviewing our goals or general sense of direction. With time, we may become able to think positively about such a crisis and be able to see it in terms of it actually having been an impetus to make some kind of fresh start. A later step is then to begin to reinvest in something that was previously taken for granted, such as a relationship with a loved one.

## *Thinking can help us to analyse a situation logically*

Once the denial and emotional turbulence of a crisis has subsided, it is helpful to attend to aspects of your crisis carefully. This includes breaking down what may seem like an overwhelming problem into smaller, more manageable chunks. From each of these chunks, you may be able to define more clearly what it is about them that is challenging and upsetting, and you may then be able to draw on past experiences, or on the experiences of those around you, to better understand what has happened. To give an example, if you were to lose your job, an initial reaction might be one of dramatic exaggeration, a stage of reacting during which you immediately think that you are a total failure and quite unemployable. But once the understandable distortions pass, you may come to see that there was actually only one area of difficulty that led to the dismissal. Also, you may be able to see ways to rectify or minimize the extent to which this interferes with getting a new job. Another good way to think about a situation follows from this, which is to break down a plan of action into small manageable steps, each one taking you closer to the solution. 'Segmenting' in this way can make things manageable, as in clarifying what you think is a reasonable goal for the day. It also helps to foster motivation, as you can see more readily how you are making progress.

## *Thinking can help by preparing us mentally*

One of the wonders of our ability to think is the capacity to imagine future scenarios. This gives us the option of inventing a number of possible challenges and rehearsing mentally how we might respond to those situations. A variety of possible coping strategies can be rehearsed in this way, and some of the likely consequences anticipated. This can then lead in to a constructive conversation with a supportive other, who can also help you to think through the most likely options for dealing with the problem that faces you. Another useful way of employing your imagination is to recall past successes in facing problems of this kind and to rehearse these in your mind. It can also help to practise talking yourself through such actions, particularly finding one or two key words or phrases that you can use to help you cope. This may include focusing on each little step that you need to take, or in giving yourself a mental pep talk to encourage you to persist in your coping efforts.

### Thinking can help us to find a purpose

Particularly in the case of the sudden and unexpected loss of a loved one, we may think that life is an uncontrollable and unpredictable mess. For some people, religion provides a way of giving such events some meaning. The particular belief systems that different religions provide have explicit ways of making sense of things like death and dying, and these beliefs can be a huge consolation to anyone suffering from a major loss. But our culture also provides a number of other ways of making a situation meaningful. Some proverbs capture a number of these beliefs, as in 'what doesn't kill you will make you stronger'. In this sense, a popular belief is that hardship is character-forming. Although unfortunate, hardship gives us the opportunity to rise above ourselves and become in some sense a 'better' person.

### Thinking helps us to take a more favourable view of reality

Once we have accepted that something terrible, such as the loss of a loved one, has happened, it is important that we try to think about the situation positively. It is one of the marvels of human nature that, no matter how dire things are, people usually manage to find something favourable in the situation. Popular strategies include reminding ourselves that things could actually be worse, or seeing ourselves as relatively well off – at least compared to others who may have suffered similar fates. The third popular way of thinking positively is to focus on something good that might emerge from the situation.

Research indicates that there is considerable variety in the ways that people manage to think about something unfortunate in a positive way. For example, in caring for a partner who has become chronically ill, one might start to see the caring as a way of repaying that person for all their help and support over the many years of the relationship. Or we may see such caring as a duty or a moral obligation, resulting in our feeling better about the situation. In the case of the mid-life crisis, similar forms of positive thinking can be identified. One of our stories, that of Mike, was a crisis that revolved around the realization that 'life was too short' to go on with a pointless, unsatisfactory marriage:

*Although the bust-up of my marriage was, of course, a terribly sad event, it was also the end of something that needed to end. Although it put pressure on our children, who are both now in their early twenties, I could see that this wasn't altogether a terrible thing for them either. This would give them the necessary push that would launch them off on their own voyages. At the same time, my ex-wife and I would also be able to change course and pursue journeys that were far more important to both of us than the old one. It was time for us to move off in different directions, and this thought comforted me, as it helped to make some kind of sense of the whole thing.*

### Thinking can help you to act

Of course, the examples of how thinking can help that I have given so far are all of the adaptive or positive kind, but a lot of our thinking is not nearly so positive in practice. Indeed, the most common coping strategies that people use focus on ways of avoiding or escaping from reality! In essence, thinking that denies or minimizes the importance of a crisis is likely to also minimize our efforts at dealing with the situation. More often than not, it is direct action that actually makes things better.

There are a variety of so-called *defence mechanisms*. One is 'intellectualization', which is a form of avoiding difficult realities by adopting a distant or philosophical perspective, one that may be devoid of the normal emotions that would normally accompany the problem. A similar example is 'rationalization', which entails trying to find a way of explaining away some action that we have taken and regret. Another kind of problematic thinking has been called 'resigned acceptance'. This means coming to terms with a situation and accepting it the way that it is, as in deciding that something can't be altered and that we must submit to our particular fate. As a result, we may disengage from a stressful situation and attempt to focus on more pleasing thoughts. It is a fatalistic belief system in which something is seen as inevitable or governed by some greater power than ourselves. On this view, we just have to resign and accept that things have to be the way they are. But resigned acceptance doesn't always prevent us from taking some action to deal with problems. It may be adaptive in the short term, keeping us going in the face of extreme stress. Then, when times are better, we can move on to more effective coping strategies, like enlisting social support from friends, to help with thinking through ways of dealing with the problem.

## Thinking can help you to 'be'

Thinking is clearly a wonderful thing, but we have to recognize the risk of 'paralysis by analysis' – in other words, thinking ourselves into even greater confusion. An obvious alternative is to try to switch the thinking off, by getting busy with some distracting activity. But there is a better way of thinking that can equally well free us from our self-imposed mental torture. This may be best understood by contrasting it with our normal way of thinking. Typically, our minds are occupied with thoughts about what we ought to be doing, how we wish things were going, whether we are making sufficient progress, what may explain our poor progress, and chastising ourselves for not doing a better job. We are focused on the current problem and evaluating our success, and we are probably fully preoccupied with the outcomes or results that we want to achieve. In short, the sought-after ends justify the rather driven means – if it works, it'll do nicely. To skip back to 'context' for a moment, it is not too surprising that we should think like this, as we live in a society where this way of being is highly valued, where being busy and 'multi-tasking' is expected. Can you hack it? You bet, just watch this!

The alternative to this 'doing' mode of living is a 'being' mode, and pretty much everything that is true of 'doing' is turned on its head in the 'being' approach. Thus, in place of a constant obsession with achieving goals, there is a focus on the *process* of how we live each moment, with the goal then becoming the 'right' way of going about things. This may mean slowing down to perform a task with care and full attention, or it may mean attending to how what we are doing affects others, as in how a conversation is unfolding. As this example indicates, any goals are likely to relate to non-material things, such as helping to support or empower someone else, rather than seeking to strengthen our own power base. The aims include accepting things as they are, and allowing things to happen without opposition or pressure. Also, when we evaluate how it's all going, we will be most interested in 'soft' indicators of progress, like how it's making us feel to be in this 'being' state. We are looking for things like a release of energy: experiencing things with greater richness, freshness, and simple, child-like pleasure. There is a direct or immediate sense of contact with what we are doing, and a welcome disregard for the passage of time. We are, as they say in sporting circles, 'playing out of our heads', immersed and fascinated with what we are doing in the present, the 'here and now'.

This 'being' mode is a truly peak experience, a time when we have an altered state of consciousness. Not only is the experience great, but the realization that such an experience is possible by healthy, natural means is a big bonus, as it says something positive about our potential. The recipe for this state of being is not particularly complicated. In fact, it is so simple (in theory) that it tends to be dismissed as nonsense by anyone in a 'doing' mode (which probably includes most of us, most of the time!). It revolves around having the right focus and the courage to immerse yourself in it, without all the usual running commentaries telling you to get back to business. In sport it is called 'the inner game' and consists of recognizing what is working well that is under our control, identifying what we need to do to reproduce it, staying concentrated on this (as opposed to getting concerned about the score), and going with it wholeheartedly.

However, in reality it is actually very difficult to do these seemingly simple things, as our mind normally works in the opposite, 'outer game' way (as in attending to our technique or the score). In particular, our media-rich culture encourages poor concentration, in terms of switching attention rapidly from one thing to the next (e.g. 'surfing' the television channels), and it also promotes quick fixes. The best alternatives I know of are the so-called Eastern ways of cultivating the right focus – such as yoga and meditation. In meditation, one spends what seems to our Western minds like ages simply attending to one thought or image, noticing – but not getting swept up in – the endless stream of our conscious mind. As a result, after a few minutes we can start to calm our minds down and attend better to simple acts of being, such as our breathing. With practice we can achieve a greater mental skill, which is the ability to 'distance' ourselves from the stream of thought in our mind. This state does not stop the 'doing' thoughts, but rather allows us to note and accept them without getting caught up in them. We can observe the stream without getting sucked back into it.

Such formal disciplines teach us a lot about just how much we tend to be wrapped up in 'doing', and, with considerable practice, can lead us into spending more time in a 'being' mode. But there are also simple, informal ways to sample 'being'. In fact, we occasionally all do so without any effort. I refer to such experiences as being on 'auto-pilot' when driving or performing some other routine task, or the 'reveries' and 'daydreaming' that may arise when we are really relaxed. These states at least switch off the 'doing' mode. To switch on 'being', we need to follow the 'inner game' guidelines, as in spending some time each day attending closely to how it feels in our muscles to perform an action (kinaesthetic awareness). Or we could reflect on the stream of our conscious mind, to better realize just what is driving us into 'doing'. (See 'Things to Try' at the end of this chapter.)

Here is a part of John's story, a sporting tale that may help to illuminate the 'being' mode:

*I was given a tape to listen to by a sports psychologist, but was highly sceptical. Having had my share of coaching, I didn't believe the grand claims that the lender of the tape was making for some simple 'inner game' benefits. I was also reluctant to listen to it before my first-ever final. But in the end I did give it a whirl. At first I thought that it was just a simple pep-talk – 'you can do it' and all that. But after listening to the advice on how to concentrate while playing, I got really interested and gave it a try. In practising for the final it seemed like I could switch from thinking the usual things about tactics and the score to just flowing, just letting the 'inner me' play the game for sheer fun. In the final I experienced an amazing feeling. Instead of 'choking' on anxiety, I got completely immersed in the feelings connected with playing the game and lost all track of the score. I got a surprise when, after what seemed like no time at all, my opponent said something about 'let's just get it over with'. Afterwards I stayed in this lovely cocoon for some time before I returned to Earth!*

## *What can reflection add?*

The different ways of thinking that I have just summarized will tend to go together in different combinations. For instance, we may typically start with a negative thought about something – such as this is not our problem, so somebody else should take responsibility for dealing with it. Then we may review things and decide that we should after all do something, followed perhaps by some action. While men and women have somewhat different ways of thinking about stressful events, the differences seem to be relatively slight. Some research suggests that when men start thinking about dealing with problems, their approach is typically concerned with direct action to resolve the matter. Women, by contrast, tend to focus on the emotional and social options. For example, women may spend considerable time worrying about the emotional impact of something that they said or did, which is tied into how others may see them as a result. They are also typically more likely to draw on the help of other people, and to express their emotions to them in their attempts to cope. However, these differences between men and women are by no means clear-cut and ever present. As touched on in Chapter 1, differences in our temperaments and in our personalities will quite probably have a stronger effect on how we think about our situation than does our gender. Another crucial determinant of whether or not our thinking patterns help us to address our mid-life crisis is simply whether or not we give sufficient time and effort to the process. This brings us on to the issue of reflection.

Much that has been written about the mid-life crisis suggests that one of its defining features is as a major stage of life review. Reassessment of ourselves and a general 'taking stock' of our situations dominates the accounts that exist. These various activities can be thought of as different forms of reflection, an activity of thinking that involves questioning and trying to redefine ourselves. The way in which this reflection is pursued will have a huge bearing on whether or not we make a successful adjustment, in terms of the rest of our lives.

### *Space to think straight*
The first key task of reflection is to allocate time to attend to our concerns, and it is important to concentrate on relevant aspects of

our crisis in order to give them deep and serious consideration. Persistence and care are also required so that we can shed new light on our situation. It will also help us to be more confident about the sense we are making of things. For instance, it can help us to gain perspective, to develop an overall idea of how some of the different pieces of our crisis fit together, so aiding us in understanding things better.

### Heightened awareness

As a result of actively and persistently reflecting on our situation, we will not only develop an ability to make better sense of things, we may also become better aware of the very process of our thinking. Our thought patterns normally go on without much conscious awareness, but careful reflection can reveal to us how we characteristically think things through. This may help us to realize that we are spending quite a bit of time thinking in ways that are probably not very helpful or adaptive. Examples were provided earlier, including avoiding thinking about some difficult aspect of the situation. We may notice, for instance, that our attempts to concentrate on something keep getting interrupted by other thoughts, or by a vagueness and lack of focus. These are important clues to our ways of thinking, and should help us to realize why we are struggling to think things through. This paves the way to the use of coping strategies to minimize such problems, such as writing things down or even learning how to concentrate, through such techniques as meditation. Many researchers and therapists believe that this heightened awareness is particularly important, because it helps us to gain insight into the way that we think. If we are able to understand and monitor our thinking patterns, then we are in a position to change them or to realize that we are making certain problematic assumptions or decisions. This is then the 'master' form of reflection, one that can benefit all of the others and play a huge part in our efforts to turn a mid-life crisis into a promising transition.

### Seeing the wood for the trees

I have already stressed the importance of spotting patterns in the way that we respond to situations, as in typically avoiding thinking about difficult things. The opposite of this recognition of patterns in our thinking is to be able to discriminate one thing from another. This includes being able to spot when we are, for once, *not* slipping into a familiar lifetrap, or noticing how other people manage to cope without falling into *your* lifetrap. Seeing how things are at times different also opens up a valuable view on the possibilities that are available to us. Even within our own behaviour over a short period, we may be aware of times when we cope relatively better than others. Noticing such differences and accentuating the better coping strategy is a hugely valuable way of thinking.

### Seeing over the horizon

One of the other 'master' ways of thinking is to see the implications of something. A famous dictum of education is 'only connect'. In other words, if we can link something we already know, and preferably understand well, to a new and perhaps challenging situation, then our thinking can be hugely helpful. Even if we have no particular link that we can make, reflecting can still help us to see the implications of a possible course of action, which is hugely empowering. It is, as the old proverb has it, the capacity to 'look before we leap'. It may also help us to choose between different possible courses of action, as one may carry much more important and desirable implications than the others. All of this really concerns ways of trying to associate or connect one thought with others that we have had.

### Perspective

Finally, reflection can add a sense of perspective on things, allowing us to evaluate the situation in a more balanced way. It can help us, for instance, to be more aware of how we feel about something that happened and, in particular, to assess how we managed a specific situation. With the aid of other ways of thinking about a situation, we may be able to re-evaluate our experience, hopefully in ways that validate us and guide us towards better ways of coping in the future.

One of the fascinating psychological benefits of this process is that we gain 'distance' over something that has been troubling us. This not only helps us to gain perspective, but also reduces unpleasant feelings associated with that troublesome event.

## *How should I go about reflecting?*

As already mentioned, for reflection to succeed it is necessary to give it time and space, for it requires effort and persistent concentration to see results. Some people find it helpful to structure reflection around a writing activity, such as a 'reflective diary'. Other forms of writing, such as a brief autobiography, are also helpful. More commonly, people reflect with the help of their friends, usually in a rather superficial way. It may be that, if you have a suitable friend, you can agree to adopt a more thorough approach in reflection – possibly by taking turns to help one another to reflect. Once you have some structure and can focus on reflection, it is then important to return to significant events and to replay them in your mind. Try to make the memories vivid and describe them in ways that bring the account to life for the listener (e.g. by providing a detailed account of a situation as it unfolded, in the form of a novel). It is also usually helpful to attend to the feelings that go with this account. Trying to find two or more words to capture the feelings that went along with the situation will help to bring it to life and enable someone else to grasp your experience better.

One of the most powerful ways to facilitate reflection is to raise basic questions. Again this can be done with the help of a friend, but it is also appropriate to try to clarify the questions and their answers on our own. If we are particularly well organized, these questions may cover a broad range of areas, each one gradually building up our understanding. For example, the first obvious question to raise concerns the nature of the experience or problem. Next, one asks about the situation in which it arose, followed by questions about factors that were relevant or influential. A critical step is then to ask whether the situation could have been managed any differently. Lastly, there is the business of drawing out any learning points, to guide future action. The material in the box lists these broad areas, with examples.

*Ways to guide reflection through asking important questions.*

| Major questions | Examples |
| --- | --- |
| 1 Describing the problem or experience clearly | How did I feel at the time? And what was I thinking? |
| 2 Reflecting on the experience | What was I trying to achieve? What prompted me to act the way that I did? |
| 3 Identifying influencing factors | What was going on inside my head at the time? What part did other people play in the situation? |
| 4 Coping with the situation | What was the main coping strategy that I used? What was the consequence of using this strategy? |
| 5 Learning from experience | What are my reflections on this experience now? What sense can I make of it? If this situation were to happen again, how might I cope with it differently? |

These are just some of the ways in which you might find it helpful to go about reflecting on important parts of your mid-life crisis. At the end of this chapter I will give a good example concerning reflection, in case you wish to find out more about this important way of thinking in order to cope more successfully.

## Is it all down to us?

One of the problems with all this emphasis on the way that we think is that it implies total responsibility on our part for the way that we are. While it is true that we are partly prisoners of our own minds, we are also partly prisoners of fate, and in this sense I would disagree with the Roosevelt quote that was given at the beginning of this chapter. It is common these days for society to emphasize how much will power or control each one of us has over our fate, but research and clinical experience strongly suggest otherwise. We are actually very much influenced by our context (as shown in Chapter 1). Each of us has a certain degree of power over our circumstances, but there is also a limit to what we can do to alter our fate.

Therefore if it is *not* all down to you, it is important to separate out in your own mind the things for which you should properly take responsibility, and the things over which you should accept no responsibility. Unfortunately, society repeatedly encourages us to take responsibility for things that are beyond our control, and this is because of the great emphasis on the individual that we have in our culture. In reality, we have limited power, including limited thinking power. As a result, it is more appropriate, when we reflect on our situation, to try to tease out the origins of our distress. Try to clarify what you have contributed to the situation and how others may also have made an important contribution. As a result, you will hopefully get a more accurate view of how fate and fortune may have trapped you into what appeared to be maladaptive coping. This has been referred to as *demystification* – namely, taking away from ourselves a mythical burden of responsibility for our condition. To demystify ourselves, we probably need the help of a sympathetic friend, someone who will patiently and persistently help us to understand our own relative contribution to the situation, in the context of social and physical factors. Out of this exercise should come some realization that some things are beyond our power to control and are not attributable simply to our own incompetence as a human being. This will move us away from traditional emphases on 'pulling our socks up' towards making sense of the jigsaw of life, in which we are but one piece.

So if it is not all down to you, and if you are only part of the problem, then presumably you are also only part of the solution? It follows then that one kind of action arising from demystification is to work towards changing other parts of our lives, other parts of our personal jigsaws. Particularly through working closely with others, such as in supportive self-help groups or small political groups, we may be able to access more power and have a greater influence on what happens to us. If nothing else, such solidarity with fellow sufferers may help us to realize that we are not alone, and therefore it is not all down to us that we end up seeing things like a mid-life crisis as nothing but failure on our part.

## *Summary*

Ancient philosophers and modern therapists agree that the way that we think about our predicament has a profound influence on how we respond to it. By taking an appropriately balanced and critical view of events, we can move from a situation filled with blame and ill-feeling to one in which the opportunities and possibilities of a new future become visible. In this chapter I have tried to summarize the ways of thinking that promote adjustment and that will probably help us to find a successful way out of our mid-life crisis – or help us onwards and upwards to an even more positive experience of successful transition.

In particular, I have looked at the beneficial effects of careful reflection on our situations. It is important to have space to think clearly about what is going on, and we also need space to come up with the kind of perspective that helps us to see the best way forward. I made some suggestions about enabling reflection to take place effectively. In particular, the use of questions can be helpful in making sense of what has happened and in drawing out the best options for the way forward. If in doing this we become more aware of our faulty ways of thinking, or of ways of connecting past and present ways of coping, then we can gain much from reflection.

But we must avoid inferring that, just because our own private thoughts are important, it is these thoughts that put us in the mess that we are in. Our thinking is indeed crucial, but it is not the only factor that creates a mid-life crisis, or a successful adjustment to a new period of our life. We also have to take account of the 'jigsaw' of our life, and the relatively small part that we all have the power to play. For this reason, I have drawn attention to the need to reflect in this relative way, and encouraged you to try to identify (and to share responsibility) with those external factors. None of us is an island. As ever, significant others provide us with potentially priceless assistance with this effort.

## Points to Ponder

You might like to return to the material in the box on page 61 and go through the sequence of major question areas that are spelt out there:

- Can you give different examples of the kinds of questions that are most appropriate in your situation?
- How you would like to phrase them to suit your thinking style?
- How does the exercise below ('Things to Try') help you to gain perspective and insight? Does it suggest some better ways of thinking about your mid-life crisis? (You will obviously need to come back to this question later.)

## Things to Try

Try to make more sense of something that concerns you by looking for patterns. In particular, is there something in your personality or nature that seems to 'cause' certain things to keep happening? Look for 'meaning' of this kind in relation to your crisis experience, as we all contribute something to our own predicaments. A second task is to find out how you tend to think about such patterns. For instance, you may have reacted a bit angrily and dismissively to the assertion I've just made, thinking to yourself that you are not in any way responsible for something that happened (or that you don't deserve the credit for a good outcome). Spotting such thinking patterns can help us to make sense of the lifetrap patterns that then follow. A logical analysis can then take place, helping us to do things like prepare effectively, so that we cope better with the emerging pattern in the future.

Another thing to try is careful reflection, and the material in the box on page 61 provides several questions that you might try tackling with somebody close. This can also aid your self-understanding and a review of your coping strategies.

Lastly, you might try some simple concentration exercises in order to heighten your awareness of the 'stream' of your mind. Try shutting your eyes and counting to ten, while visualizing each number vividly. Every time you notice something else coming into your mind and distracting you from this task, start again at 1. If you reckon you've done it straight away, you are either a devotee of meditation or you simply have not been focusing all of your mind on the images! Or you discount other interfering thoughts, as you can still 'see' the numbers. You should be aiming for a continuous, unblemished image of the numbers, for a pure 10 seconds of 'being'. Most likely, if you are honest about the interferences, you will not be able to succeed. But this task will teach you about your mind and about the struggle to 'be', even for just 10 seconds! With practice, you should improve – and if you like the effect, you could go on to formal meditation.

# 5

## Changing behaviour: practical ways to manage your crisis

The quality of life is determined by its activities.

(Aristotle)

One of the main ways to cope with the kinds of problems that arise during a mid-life transition is the use of behavioural approaches. In other words, by taking action we can alter how we think and feel about difficulties, and we can also try to remove sources of stress. Often, taking appropriate action is in fact the most effective way to change negative thinking or unpleasant feelings. It can be much harder than changing the way we think, but also much more powerful.

In this chapter, I will be describing three broad ways in which we can act. These are to take problem-solving action, to look for new sources of reward in life, and to seek out social support. These behavioural acts complement the ways of thinking differently, as described in the previous chapter. Indeed, wise action is based on careful thought. It also allows us to test out our beliefs and fears, so improving our thinking. This cycle of thought and action also dovetails with the next chapter, which is concerned with emotionally processing material that we need to recognize and address during transitions.

One of the main triggers to a mid-life crisis is a change at work, so this will be a central feature of this chapter. Problems in the workplace are a growing cause of distress for middle-aged people, partly because of our fear of becoming obsolescent. The restructuring of companies, mergers, or simply changes in management itself, can all lead to dramatic and unforeseen changes in our job. This is in marked contrast to the kind of stability that a middle-aged person typically encountered when they first started their working life. Modern society has moved to 'downsizing' and to an increased emphasis on computerization and 'skill mixing'. These kinds of forces can lead to an experienced and very able middle-aged employee becoming much more readily devalued or even dismissed.

A further problematic aspect of this stage of life is that this slippery work slope has to be tackled at a time when many middle-aged people will be aiming for a higher position. After all, it is a natural and socially desired thing to do: to seek greater status, responsibility and pay, to become a senior member of the organization, and to realize our potential as employees.

Active ways of dealing with such tricky employment situations, or with early retirement, require good active coping strategies for a successful transition. However, active coping is relevant to all kinds of stress associated with the mid-life crisis. Therefore, please treat references to the workplace as simply providing an example of how such coping strategies can be useful.

## What does it mean to take problem-solving action?

Problem-solving action is the behaviour we use to deal directly with aspects of our crisis. It includes making plans jointly with others, dedicating ourselves to making a success of things, as well as using different strategies to obtain our goals (e.g. by altering our approach to important relationships).

### Break activities down into small steps (staying in your 'zone')

Particularly when we are feeling stuck or emotionally uncomfortable (e.g. feeling resentment about not being promoted at work), it can be hugely beneficial to break down our general response or intended outcome into small steps. This process of analysing what you are trying to do is useful in defining sub-goals, in improving the chances of achieving them, and in quickly raising morale. How safe or confident you feel in taking these steps is also an important consideration, and it would be wise to introduce some early steps that will build in success. A graded, gradual approach often works best, but even when it fails this degree of careful planning will at least help us to spot where we are falling down.

An important part of careful goal-setting is that we should always be operating in ways that we feel are comfortable. Over-extending ourselves is likely to be problematic and risky. Even world champions learn to work within their 'zones of optimal functioning'. Therefore, when you are taking action to deal with the next step in your transition, ensure that you stay in your zone. Strangely enough, this can often produce the 'personal best' performances.

### Emphasizing the positive

Related to breaking things down into safe and manageable steps is the business of emphasizing your strengths and recognizing what is likely to receive a positive reaction from others. That is, in thinking about the steps that you might wish to take towards solving a problem, it can be useful to distinguish between things that give you a sense of pleasure or mastery, versus those that create anxiety and lead to you feeling deskilled or incompetent. For instance, if you function best in face-to-face communication, focus on rehearsing this strength. And while we may have a good idea in advance about which steps will work best for us, the key is to watch carefully for the reactions of others to each progressive step. To return to the example of the workplace, a compliment from a boss or a 'thank you' from a client is important evidence that the change that you are working towards will be successful in the longer term. Once a step receives support from significant others, it also has the benefit of increasing our sense of control and progress.

### Rehearsing to improve performance

If a step goes wrong or if you think that the next step is likely to prove difficult, another way to use active coping is to practise taking that step. We can do this with a friend or on our own in private, and it may also be useful to practise in a graded way – that is, start by rehearsing under ideal conditions then move on to more difficult ones. A really systematic rehearsal will even anticipate a 'worst possible scenario', so that our confidence in dealing with the real-life situation is as high as possible.

We can also help this process of rehearsal by talking ourselves through a task, *sub-vocally*. This means that we talk to ourselves in our heads, in a way that guides us through the task, drawing attention to key aspects and giving ourselves praise for progress.

A further variation on the rehearsal theme is to imagine the steps that have to be taken. Again, this can be done in its own graded way, starting by imagining dealing with the situation in a straightforward way, and leading up to more difficult scenarios. By taking these sorts of preparatory actions we can boost our confidence and increase the likelihood of success.

Yet another way to rehearse for a successful performance is to carry out a practice session. The idea of role-playing is frightening to most people, but if set up carefully and conducted in the right spirit, it can provide the most confidence-boosting and helpful preparation of all. Some of the best role-plays are quite natural extensions of a conversation. In this way, once you have perhaps agreed the next step with a friend or work colleague, you might then start to practise that step with that particular individual. The atmosphere should be relaxed but realistic, so that the practice is useful to the eventual action. Another advantage of role-play is that it can be repeated until you feel confident, and the other person can provide feedback to strengthen your competence.

### Setting the scene

In support of things like rehearsal is the need for careful attention to the social and physical context. Socially, many people find it helpful to make a commitment to some action. This acts as a strong lever, particularly when followed up by some kind of ongoing progress review. Another way in which the social aspect can be helpful is indirectly enlisting the help of someone else in dealing with a problematic situation. Again, this can build on things like role-play and rehearsal, so that you share the next step together.

In terms of the physical surroundings, it can also be helpful at times to make sure that the way things are organized physically is as helpful as possible to the task in question. If this is a workplace issue, ensuring that a particular conversation takes place in a quiet part of the building, for instance, is conducive to successful task completion. Similarly, taking somebody that you wish to talk to into a different, more helpful setting may be useful (e.g. if you wish to have a quiet word about a problem, you might ask the person to join you for a cup of tea in a secluded part of the staff canteen).

### Faking it

Another surprisingly effective technique for some people is to simply act as if things were already resolved in the way that they had hoped. On this thinking, we act in a way that fits with how we would like to feel, or would like to be regarded by others. This can be thought of as another example of rehearsal, except that it is done in real life and skips to the final desired behaviour. Obviously, this is an unwise approach if that final step is too far removed from your present approach, but it might be worth a try for some smaller problems – or perhaps even in relation to one of the steps. Again, this could be rehearsed with the help of a friend. Perhaps the best way to think about this is in terms of a commitment to act in ways that you think are going to be most successful.

### Distracting and avoiding

Although these behaviours are normally to be discouraged, because they tend not to address the problem, there may be times when they are appropriate. For instance, when we fail to get any relief or progress from the above techniques, or where we are faced with a challenge that is currently beyond our powers to resolve, then these methods may be justified.

Distraction behaviours include focusing on more pleasant things so that we can keep functioning when faced with something un-pleasant. For example, if our work colleague is irritating us, we may function more effectively and be able to return to dealing with that irritation by temporarily focusing on some interesting part of the job in hand – that is, by 're-focusing'. We may also find it helpful occasionally *not* to attend too closely to a challenging task. In this way, concentrating on the next step, or on some useful action that we can take now, will help us to keep moving in the direction of progress. Other examples include simply doing something totally different – such as going for a walk or to see a film.

Avoiding problematic people or situations is also a short-term option. This may mean going out of our way to avoid a difficult individual, or simply limiting the time or the nature of our contact with them. More positively, we could try to ignore the irksome things about someone while at the same time letting them know how much we appreciate the more acceptable parts of them. For example, somebody who is almost always critical can be given minimal encouragement while they are actually criticizing, but then given far more affirming attention when they are being positive.

### Developing new skills

In keeping with this example, there is no limit to our competence in dealing with people, whether at work or elsewhere. One fundamental skill, whether about people or anything else, is the ability to carry out a 'problem-solving' analysis. This involves defining a particular problem carefully and then generating some options for its solution. The best of these options is then selected and implemented, leading to an evaluation of its success. Incidentally, this is a good example of how the way we cope through our thinking is inextricably tied in with how we act.

Once an option for solving a problem has been defined in this way, the next step may be to develop competence in carrying out this option. A good example is assertiveness, a vital skill in the workplace and elsewhere. So, for example, our goal may have been to express a negative feeling to someone and the best option for doing this may have been determined as telling them how you would feel about something that upsets you on a good day and a bad day. The 'bad day' example allows you to say how you really feel, enabling you to express the feeling and to get a reaction from the other person. Often this is surprisingly affirming, as the other person may already have sensed that this was how you were feeling.

## Taking good care of yourself

In the event of something as distressing as redundancy or premature retirement, it is tempting to retreat into recrimination and negativity. Meanwhile, you can fail to take sufficient care of yourself, thus exacerbating the problem. Therefore, it is important to take the time to rest and recover. Take exercise too, which improves your health and gives you a good feeling. Take care also of your appearance, in terms of the way you dress or present yourself. Generally just getting out and about, especially in the countryside or parks, can help to reinvigorate and reorientate you to the tasks that lie ahead. It can provide a valuable perspective as well. Try simultaneously to minimize your use of the kind of avoidance coping that undermines how you appear or act. Alcohol use, late nights, the use of recreational or other drugs, excessive caffeine, and other similar habits are all undermining and limit your ability to respond effectively to the challenge of transition. Instead of making yourself feel worse, do what you can to do those things that make you feel and act more effectively, whether that is exercise or healthy eating habits. And if this is hard to implement, why not treat this lifestyle aspect as the 'problem' that requires the kind of steps that I have listed so far in this chapter?

## Creating your own personal space

In the turmoil of transition, it is only too easy to lose the time and space for considered reflection. Therefore, a key action is to create the appropriate time and place for you to reflect thoughtfully on how your choice of actions and your appraisal of how things are progressing. This may be a particular physical place where you regularly go to reflect (e.g. a café or park), and it does need to involve committing a regular time for reflection. Indeed, there is a need to give yourself 'permission' to be inactive, to have time out.

A warning, though: it is important to let those who care about you know that you are doing this for personal space reasons and not because you are trying to distance yourself or are rejecting them. For instance, this can be presented to them as a 'refuelling' activity, designed to strengthen rather than weaken such important relationships. Getting sufficient general rest and satisfactory sleep can be thought of as an extension of this personal space. Sleep is hugely important to our ability to think straight and to act effectively.

## Learning to relax

One way to help yourself to rest and sleep is to learn how to relax systematically, to treat it as a 'skill' to be acquired. Such relaxation is not the same as taking a holiday or listening to some soothing music; systematic approaches to relaxation are a way of learning how to calm mind and body. There are a number of self-help tapes and booklets on the market to help with this skill, most of them teaching you how to tense and relax the different muscle groups of the body so as to heighten your awareness of your level of activation, and to strengthen your ability to lower such activation to the point where you can readily go to sleep. Related techniques include yoga and meditation, and these may be more appealing to some people than a systematic approach to relaxation.

## Separating form from function

These different approaches to relaxation illustrate a key point: the fact that there are many ways to achieve your goal, at least in theory. The ways in which they differ are really unimportant – what matters is that they work, and that they end up leaving you feeling relaxed. Feeling relaxed is then the 'function', purpose or goal of such 'forms' of relaxing such as meditation. The implication of this point is that this distinction can help us to see issues and manage our active coping more effectively.

Take the example of 'social support' (more to follow, in the next section). Support can take a bewildering range of forms, from the clear-cut message of support from a close friend to a passing remark from a stranger – and it may happen once or be repeated endlessly. These are mere details, to be clearly distinguished from the effect that this has on you – the function that it serves in your life. In terms of social support, the critical functions it tends to serve are such things as a sense of belonging, feeling valued, and being understood (Chapter 1 also discussed support functions).

Therefore, when reflecting on your actions or planning the next steps, try to separate the 'form' of events from their 'function'. By focusing on the important functions, we are better placed to act wisely.

### Seeing bad situations for what they are

Lastly, it is important to recognize that sometimes the problem lies elsewhere. It is all too common these days to be told that it is the individual who is at fault. However, it is often the situation that needs to change, not the individual. Work is as good an example of this as anything else, and you can probably readily think of changes that should really take place within the workplace, rather than within the workers. An example that comes to mind for me is the lack of clear and consistent communication from above about the current goals of the organization. Rather, we hear varying versions and are given different priorities by various people within the organization. The result can often be that the individual is left feeling inadequate or 'stressed out', when in fact it is the organization itself that needs to 'get its act together'.

Collaborating with others to get management to acknowledge its responsibility in the situation and taking collective action to address problems constructively are important behavioural coping strategies. And if all else fails, recognizing, with the help of colleagues, that the situation is down to the workplace and not the workers at least creates a sense of solidarity and protects us against excessively 'owning' such problems.

*An illustration*
Mike's personal story is relevant to some of these coping strategies:

> *I was 47 and had decided, together with my mate, that by the time I was 50 I would have achieved my career ambition. However, although I worked harder than ever, it seemed that the goal was beyond my reach and felt out of my control. It began to be most frustrating and dispiriting. I decided I couldn't keep on banging my head on the old brick wall. One of the first things I did was to take myself off to an evening class and learned how to meditate. The approach was that of Zen, which carried the benefit of introducing me to a very different outlook on life. Fortunately, the meditation and the outlook could be used during the working day to help me feel more relaxed and in control. I was then better able to break down the large goal I had set myself into manageable chunks, which could then be tied to particular time points. I then enlisted the help of my pal in imagining some of the situations that I'd have to deal with and practising some handling strategies with him. This combination of methods made me feel much more in control and may have contributed to my eventual success.*

## How can social support help?

Social support is of profound importance to our functioning and our well-being (as outlined in Chapter 1). Just as we might say that (for men in particular) our job defines us, so we might say that social support makes us who we are. We are not an island, and we gain a strong sense of who we are from those around us. We also get a sense of direction from our loved ones, and help in moving towards our goals. By obtaining information from others about the nature of the problem and possible ways of coping with it, by obtaining practical assistance, by enjoying the emotional support of others and by simply feeling that we belong, we are drawing on social support. Mike's story (above) illustrates this central role of support. The section on 'form and function' draws out just why such help matters to our well-being.

It follows that the actions we take to strengthen such support are crucially important. This includes actions taken to avoid or control 'anti-social support' (e.g. being criticized or rejected), or to address the feeling that we have no support at all. Our social support influences how we feel in ourselves and shapes our effectiveness in addressing our transition problems. In fact, support helps in many ways, as this list shows:

### Help in reviewing things

By enlisting the help of close, confiding friends and family members, we can gain good feedback on our efforts to act effectively; and being aware of how our efforts are perceived is a crucial part of any coping strategy. Unfortunately, when we are distressed, this capacity can go haywire, but having the view of a relatively independent, objective ally to improve our self-review can make all the difference. For instance, if you are pursuing a plan and becoming dispirited, reviewing what has happened and the sense that you are making of your own progress can be surprisingly illuminating and put you back on course.

### Bandaging the cracks

Coping with something like a redundancy is likely to cause most people significant distress. The tension at home can become a further complication, putting pressure on relationships at the very time that they are most important. It is therefore crucial to discuss the feelings that are being evoked with your partner or other close friends. The aim is to gain their understanding and perspective, but also to enlist their help in 'papering over the cracks'. That is, social supporters can help to keep us operational and sane, and they can help us to deal with any despair or self-reproach by such reactions as recognizing our adaptive coping.

### Validating our experience

One of the most striking things that we can experience in relation to a stressful life event is how the same sort of stress is experienced by others. This strong 'universality' effect is partly due to our tendency to be secretive about our experience. This may be in part because society teaches us, especially men, to be strong and not to show 'weakness'. But it is also due to the powerful realization that we are not necessarily alone: it is actually common to find that others who have gone through a comparable experience have similar perceptions and feelings to ours. By joining a self-help group, or simply taking the opportunity to check such perceptions at appropriate social opportunities, we can validate our own experience. The internet may also provide us with some helpful opportunities to check out and validate our experience, thereby obtaining further social support.

### Providing assistance

Another general way in which social support can help is by directly furnishing us with materials or aid. If we are able to borrow a piece of equipment or even to enlist someone's practical help, we are better able to take effective action. There may also be the bonus of feeling good about our friends and supporters, and about our implied worth as an individual. Of course, asking for help does not come easily to most people. If this is true of you, it may make support-seeking a suitable goal for you. As we've mentioned before, men in particular may see help-seeking as a sign of weakness, of powerlessness. The trading of practical help or materials, though, may be one way to offset the discomfort and to get on with the vital business of enlisting valuable help.

### Feeling supported

This is not the same as the preceding point, in that what is of paramount importance, regardless of any help or resources that others provide, is how we come to feel about ourselves as a result of other people. Feeling that we belong and that others value our contribution to their lives contributes to this sense of being supported. Being understood and feeling that you understand others is also vital (empathy). By contrast, being disagreed with, arguments, criticisms and general disapproval will undermine our sense of being supported and belonging. Clearly, then, we need to take action to minimize criticism and rejection and to maximize support and acceptance. We may need to work on our relationships so that we are seen as understanding and supportive, rather than as irritating and critical. A good motto in all of this is: 'as ye sow, so shall ye reap'. If you want others to treat you in a certain way, it is not a bad idea to begin by treating them in just that self-same way yourself! Do you make yourself available when your friends are in difficulty? Do you try to cheer them up when they are sad and worried? Do you encourage them to confide in you? Are you able to show empathy and understanding, even if you disapprove of some of the things that they have been doing?

When Teena's marriage fell apart, social support was central. Indeed, it could be said that it was partly her husband's lack of support for her that led Teena to walk out on him. Three aspects of social support stand out in this story – 'validation' of Teena's view of the problem, and the provision of 'practical' and 'emotional' support, by one of her friends in particular:

> *I told two close friends that I'd left Tom and they both knew why, before I'd said anything. One asked me 'Was he drinking?' and the other indicated that she had also picked up the smell of alcohol on his breath. I felt that they understood me and were completely behind me. Once I found a place to stay, one of them came round every day, bringing little things like food (for a while I couldn't face going out).*

## Can seeking alternative rewards be valuable?

Even under normal circumstances, one of the most popular ways that we cope with stress is to engage in well-developed avoidance and escape activities. These are many and various, but serve to either minimize, totally block out, or to terminate stress by finding some way out of the situation. When we are faced with more demanding stressors, the temptation to escape and avoid is all the stronger. Common and damaging strategies include the abuse of alcohol and the persistent avoidance of the various tasks entailed by a life transition. This may be as simple as ensuring that a difficult issue is discussed and resolved with someone, rather than 'parking' the issue and hoping it will somehow go away.

As noted earlier, when we are faced with a situation about which we can do little, avoidance behaviours make a lot of sense and may even be best in the long run. An example would be caring for somebody who has a major physical or mental problem, one that is unlikely to improve (e.g. dementia). Escape actions may also be for the best when they extract us from a situation that is no longer tenable (e.g. a relationship or job where we have tried our best to rectify it, but in vain).

By escaping or avoiding we are free to pursue alternative rewards in life. This may include the work we do to replace losses, or to create new sources of satisfaction in life. This may be based on making plans and changing our direction. Setting appropriate, specific and short-term goals is another example of this planning activity. A variation on this theme is to try to move into different social circles or situations, so that the activities that you find rewarding are prioritized. Mike's meditation class is a case in point. John had a similar approach:

*I felt I needed something fresh and different, so I decided to take up sport again, but a new one. I decided to try badminton, partly because I knew one of the people who played regularly from work, and partly as I had heard that a good bunch of people went there. I suppose I was as interested in the social side as the sport.*

In the field of work, a typical example may be to redirect our efforts towards something that, as a result of the life-crisis experience, becomes a priority. Such a new direction may be to channel our energy into such things as helping others who have suffered or struggled with the experience that we have gone through. Practical examples might be sharing information, raising funds to support some suitable activity, or acting as a counsellor or helper, redirecting others. Here are some more examples:

### Making realistic self-assessments

The first major milestone in a transition is fully recognizing that something is at an end, and only when we close the old can we properly begin something new. In this sense, if we have a difficult situation it is important to recognize clearly what has gone wrong and to adjust our plans or goals accordingly. To take the example of the workplace again, it may be that following a mid-life crisis you prioritize different things in life. This may compromise your willingness to work as vigorously as previously towards the old work objectives. You may decide that it is not realistic to maintain the previous level of effort, and that a more sensible set of goals is needed. Establishing what those goals are, preferably with line managers and colleagues, is an important activity that both acknowledges that transition needs to take place and directs our efforts towards a more satisfying goal.

## Taking time to do the job properly

The above makes it sound like a simple matter of pausing and gathering our thoughts before redirecting our efforts. However, in practice it is unlikely to be so smooth and straightforward. The transition will entail some psychological pain and discomfort, and this will tend to encourage us to use avoidance and escape activities. This will be distractions to avoid thinking about some of the more difficult decisions we might need to make. For this reason, it is important to go about the business of self-assessment and defining a fresh direction carefully. A good way to ensure this is to talk things through very slowly and deliberately with a close confiding person, such as a partner or close family friend.

Another good coping strategy to buy time is to set up temporary arrangements that give us the space to process and decide sensibly, as in getting a temporary job while you gather your thoughts and determine what might be the next best course of action in your career. Similarly, you may come to arrangements at home or at work to carry on in a different way until something is resolved. For example, this might even include some special or compassionate leave from the workplace, or a placement in some related part of the business.

## Looking after ourselves

For some people, part of the new direction is actually to take far more care of their own well-being, whether this is through a better diet, taking more exercise, enjoying a favourite hobby, or simply getting sufficient sleep. Even if only on a temporary basis, such lifestyle changes can invigorate our planning activity and energize our imagination, so that ideas that might otherwise have not been entertained are thought through creatively.

It is important to note that lifestyle changes can be both the plan and the action, redirecting us away from a possibly damaging job or situation towards a focus on our own well-being and on the things that give us pleasure (e.g. outdoor hobbies such as gardening or walking).

## *Doing things differently*

A less extreme example is to try to alter the way that we go about things, whether this is becoming more relaxed, more thoughtful about the choices that we make, attentive and responsive to the needs of others, developing the kind of social support we get, or in other ways trying to feel better about what we do. If nothing else, this change of emphasis may well help the process of self-assessment and review. One way in which it does this is to add perspective and some 'distance' from the familiar ways of handling things. It may therefore make us more aware of something that we tend to do that may be counterproductive to our happiness (e.g. not giving others enough of our time, so that they feel alienated or resentful towards us, in turn lowering our quality of life).

## *Changing others*

Logically, as this example shows, you might not only attempt to change your lifestyle, but also try to change how others relate to you. This can be a direct result of the changes you make, as in giving people more time and attention, and observing the benefits that follow. More typically, such changes involve moving to different environments, whether at work or in terms of where we live, so that we get a fresh start and can create a situation that is more likely to be pleasing. This might mean sacrificing a better paid and more prestigious job for something less well rewarded financially, but that actually brings greater satisfaction at a time when money is not everything.

## *Making it happen*

The initial stages of self-assessment, review and planning a fresh track in life are often accompanied by euphoria or a strong sense of relief, as we sense that we might be moving out of an aversive situation to something far more satisfying. But it is all too common for this initial period to be followed by difficulties, whether at home or at work. For instance, if you are unemployed or newly retired, after a few weeks the pressure to take action and move on to a new stage will become considerable, both from inside yourself and from friends and family. This is inevitable if you are truly taking a fresh course, as this will challenge and possibly even threaten some of these people, as you are effectively 'de-stabilizing' their lives. As a result, they will want to make their own coping efforts to place you back in your old position.

For example, it would be very hard for your partner to tolerate more than a few weeks of apparent indolence, as you do the necessary reflection and self-assessment work, gradually building plans for a fresh direction in life. It is therefore vital to communicate with exceptional clarity and effectiveness if you are to carry these people with you and engage them in the work, so that they also feel energized and positive about the new direction. One way to do this would be drawing out as clearly as possible as many of the likely mutual benefits of such a change as possible, part of a 'win-win' approach. Cultivating new relationships is probably going to be a vital part of this effort, particularly in trying to make contact with others in a similar position to yourself. Trying to boost friendships and generally getting out and about will aid the personal 'feel good' factor and also help to develop greater awareness and perspective, helping you to make better judgements.

### Getting help

Some people will find it helpful to join a self-help group or at least to access information designed to give guidance or direction at this stage (e.g. in turning to a new career). Reading is a great source of help in these situations as it can provide a variety of specific tips, but also a more general understanding of the situation that you are in and the options for a fresh direction.

Some also find they need a counsellor, therapist or 'career coach'. Such people can provide, individually or in a group situation, a more personalized and responsive approach, to supplement what we can get from social support and books.

### Increase the things that give you pleasure

In the middle of a difficult period, we may tend to play down or even ignore the simple pleasures in life; so to help establish a healthy balance, take time to engage in activities that you enjoy. This will tend to improve your mood and, with it, your problem-solving action. If you are feeling bold, you could even try increasing the pleasurable activities until whole days become pleasurable!

## Believe!

To succeed in any of these ways of finding a new direction we have to commit wholeheartedly to the effort and have sufficient belief or 'blind faith' to see it through – and this is never more true than in the characteristically turbulent early periods of transition. It seems to be a law of nature that the initial part of change is troubled and turbulent, causing us to feel de-stabilized or even 'disintegrated'. This stage seems to be a necessary start to the process of making a transition, just as an athlete needs to feel uncomfortably anxious before a competition event. In such a difficult time, transition tends to be a huge personal struggle, and it may help to remind yourself that this sort of de-stabilization is necessary for you to move on – it creates the conditions for change. Therefore, try to believe firmly in the path that you have defined out of your mid-life crisis, especially when it hurts. One of the worst possible forms of avoidance or escape would be to abandon the dream, before it has had time to succeed.

## *Summary*

Changing the practical ways that we act to deal with the demands of the mid-life transition represents the single most powerful means of coping effectively. In this chapter I have highlighted three broad ways of coping through our actions. These are:

- to redefine our goals and seek alternative rewards
- to maximize social support
- to take problem-solving action

The last of these included a considerable number of coping strategies, such as breaking down goals into small, graded steps and seeking as much pleasure and mastery as possible from attempts to grapple with our problems.

Obviously, to be successful these coping strategies need to be adapted to suit your own personal style – and this is no simple cliché. I have stressed in this chapter that it is vital, when trying to find a new path towards life satisfaction, to pause and reflect carefully on how we tend to avoid and escape from certain crucial things in our life. It is equally necessary for us to gain perspective and move slowly into the implementation of a plan, staying within our own comfort zones.

One of the best ways to figure out whether we are using escape and avoidance is to ask: 'What are the purposes of this behaviour?' This is like distinguishing between somebody who seems to work furiously and very successfully (the 'workaholic') and the actual *function* that being a workaholic serves for that person. On the surface, this individual may seem hugely successful and be admired. However, if the actual purpose of all that energy is actually to escape from a difficult relationship at home, or from playing a full part in rearing the children, then it might be viewed more as escape, rather than the fulfilment of a life mission. In the same way, we need to distinguish between the things that might *seem* to be adaptive and helpful (but in reality are not) from those things that actually move us closer to the goals we want to achieve, whether this is in work or any other area of our lives.

In the next chapter I will go on to detail what some of these key functions are from an emotional perspective. In this sense, we want to find a direction out of the mid-life crisis that maximizes the satisfaction and fulfilment we can get out of life, while minimizing the pain.

## Points to Ponder

- Reflecting on a recent action that you have taken, can you fit it readily into the material above?
- Is it an example of 'problem-solving'?
- If not, can you see a link to the purposes ('functions') of the three broad forms of action I've described?
- Was this action typical, another manifestation of your personality?
- How will your personality tend to shape the form that your actions take?

## Things to Try

Of the tips that I have presented in this chapter, which would be the three most relevant ones for you to apply to your life at present? And of those three, how would you need to personalize the tips to make them suitable for your own style and to your own situation (e.g. your job)?

What is your social support network like – could you draw a map to show the distances between you and the main six or ten people in your life? Can you also add to this network map a symbol to show the kind of social support that those people provide? Can you distinguish between the 'form' of their support and the 'functions' that it serves in your life? An obvious point to then consider is what you might do, in terms of changing your own behaviour, to strengthen your social support? This might be to extend your network, or by working towards achieving better results from your present social group.

# 6

## Coping with your feelings

> ... thought and actions start from a single source, namely feeling.
> (Epictetus, *Discourses*)

As this quote indicates, emotions are essential to how we cope and are the essence of what it means to be a human being. Alongside our ability to use language, our emotional experiences must rank among the top human qualities. The arts can be viewed as drawing on experience to allow humans to express emotion. Often the emotions and the individual are seen as one, as in this quote from the classical composer Gustav Mahler:

> *To anyone who knows how to listen, my whole life will become clear, for any creative works and my existence are so clearly interwoven that if my life flowed as peacefully as a stream through a meadow, I believe I would no longer be able to compose anything.*

Throughout our evolution, emotions have evolved as patterns of responding to our circumstances and our experience of life, as reflected in the Mahler quote. It is believed that emotions are innate in both humans and animals, being present at birth and showing a remarkable consistency both over time and within the species. Also consistent is the purpose of emotional expression and experience, which is partly to prepare us for action, and partly to communicate to others how we are feeling. In these senses, we can see that emotions are a fundamental way in which we adapt and manage transitions through the mid-life period.

## *What are our emotions?*

Because emotional reactions are complex and quite capable of bewildering us, it is perhaps not surprising that researchers have had great difficulty in answering this question. Part of the confusion is because three closely connected threads run through our emotional experience. First, there are reflexes that have strong emotional aspects, such as the way that we respond to pain without any necessary thought. Such reactions are therefore automatic and fairly fixed responses to events. The startle reaction is another reflex, a kind of basic building block for emotion.

The second strand that underpins emotions is our physiological state. These are also responses to situations that arise automatically, as in how we feel when hungry or excited.

However, true emotions are the result of how we appraise or interpret what is going on, including our reflexes and physiological state. As emphasized in Chapter 3, everything turns on our interpretation of these stimuli. A further reason for the confusion over emotions is that, in turn, how we interpret something will potentially affect our physiological reaction. One can then see how a pattern of responding is created, for better or for worse. Take the example of speaking in public – say as a best man at a wedding, or in making a farewell speech at work. Most people feel physiological arousal of a marked kind, in terms of such sensations as a pounding heart, jelly-like knees or a dry mouth. These physical states are regulated by physiological processes. If we interpret these physical sensations as meaning that we are anxious, then we can expect those sensations to intensify. On the other hand, if we take the view, as athletes learn to do, that these physical sensations are actually part of our readiness to perform at our best, then this interpretation results in a different view of the experience and a calming that makes the individual feel ready.

As a result of this appraisal or interpretation activity, we come to feel one of a number of emotions. The list is set out in the box below, together with the kind of situation that tends to make us react in this way.

*The different kinds of emotion and their main triggers.*

| Emotions | Triggers to these emotions |
| --- | --- |
| Anger | An offence that demeans or belittles you |
| Anxiety | Being faced with uncertainty or threat; feeling out of control |
| Fright | A powerful physical 'fight or flight' reaction |
| Guilt | Breaking moral rules |
| Shame | Failing to live up to an ideal |
| Sadness | Experiencing a loss |
| Envy | Desiring things that others have |
| Jealousy | Resenting a threat to or loss of someone's affection or favour |
| Disgust | Reaction to an unacceptable or unpleasant thing |
| Happiness | Making progress towards a goal |
| Pride | Gaining credit or approval for achievement |
| Relief | Reduction in a distressing or problematic situation |
| Hope | Having grounds for optimism |
| Love | Desiring or participating in affection |
| Compassion | Identification with someone else's suffering |

Just as the way that we interpret our physiological state or other events will affect the kind of emotion that we experience, the way that we in turn respond to a growing emotion will result in different kinds of feeling reactions. Our coping strategies are crucial to this unfolding link. In this sense, feeling angry about some offence or inappropriate action that you feel someone else has taken may lead to several forms of distress or reaction. These may include numbness, loneliness and helplessness. The numbness may arise because we feel at least temporarily unable to deal with the source of our anger or indeed with the emotion of anger itself. Alternatively, if we cope by viewing the source of the anger as signifying that we are in some sense different and isolated from other people, then we may come to feel lonely. Another reaction is to view the source of the anger as something that is overwhelmingly powerful or something that we are unable to alter. A clear example of this is the anger that we may feel if diagnosed with a serious illness. We are angry because it may seem wrong in some sense for this to happen: we may feel that we have lived a good and healthy life, and so it is unfair to have such a condition. And if the condition is one that we feel or are told cannot be modified, then we will come to feel helpless. Therefore, we can see a sequence of events leading to a major emotion and to resulting distress, all of which is profoundly influenced by our coping strategies.

In this chapter I will be detailing how we can strengthen our capacity to cope through our emotional system. (I will not be emphasizing how we can change how we feel by improving our ways of thinking or behaving, as these matters are already covered in Chapters 4 and 5.) What I want to do is show how our emotional system can be an ally in our efforts to cope with a mid-life crisis; it is another string to our coping bow. And also to complement the earlier chapters, this one focuses on physical health, a major dimension of the mid-life crisis.

Around the mid-life period there are a number of inescapable physical signs of ageing. These include a general slowing down (including our nervous system and reaction times, our reflexes, and the fact that physically we take a longer period to heal or recover). A second feature is a sense of becoming weaker, again including physical brittleness and sensitivity, but also in terms of our general physical strength. Our sensory system also tends to suffer with the passage of time, as in the deterioration that is common to our hearing and to our vision. Such physical signs of ageing can be a trigger for a mid-life crisis and also a major aspect of our coping reactions (e.g. making us feel relatively helpless in responding to a physical challenge).

## How do we cope emotionally in general?

In the popular literature there are some classic examples of emotion-based coping, most of it negative. One such category is 'surrendering', which consists of negative thinking about the situation and a general sense that once life has been mismanaged, it is now pointless. Efforts to cope with a situation are seen as futile, absurd and pointless. However, individuals seen as functioning in this way usually struggle on to some kind of adjustment, and tend to attract a certain kind of sympathetic audience.

A second broad type of emotional coping is based around 'escape'. Individuals in this category are beset by concerns about various threats that are then to be avoided or, if they commence, need to be escaped from. The preoccupation is with not fully accepting how one is feeling, which is achieved by focusing attention on alternative rewards and escape mechanisms (e.g. the abuse of alcohol or drugs).

The third popular strategy is to 'counter attack'; this kind of individual also tends to deny their feelings but, rather than escaping, will turn things like anger and self-loathing towards others. They will also tend to exercise extreme control, in order to cope with what may be a rather threatened or even paranoid view of the world. There is also a need to adopt a rigid control over their own aggressive impulses, so they do not act out socially unacceptable beliefs. Unlike escapers, 'counter attackers' will typically express their discontent with the world very strongly and effectively, with the suggestion that others need to be knocked into shape. They lay responsibility for the numerous and exaggerated threats they see around them at the feet of others.

Far better than these characterizations is to try to cope emotionally in ways that recognize our own responsibility and capacity to create a better state of affairs – let's call these people 'copers'. Such types acknowledge a need for change and the importance of overcoming an unacceptable situation. They will feel a need to make a significant commitment in order to make the best possible use of their life. This includes working towards coping in ways that benefit other people, and that leave behind them positive products of their life. Also, with this type of adjustment, it is possible to reach positive feelings about work, relationships, and even about our inevitable physical decline. Such individuals have a sense of control over their fate and tend to be responsive, warm, supportive and accepting of others, even the rather challenging types discussed earlier!

## What specific ways are there of coping emotionally?

### Avoidance and escape

As noted above, a very tempting and popular way to cope emotionally is to try to 'turn off' a problem, and surveys of the British public suggest that this is the single most popular way of coping. In essence, there are two broad coping options. The first is avoidance, which involves trying not to encounter a problematic event in the first place. The second logical possibility is to try to escape from such events if they are unavoidable. Both of these options serve to temporarily terminate an unacceptable or unpleasant stressor. In caricature terms, this is the ostrich-like reaction to stress, bringing temporary relief – but probably not a very wise approach to coping. Researchers and clinicians tend to classify avoidance and escape as 'maladaptive' forms of coping, by contrast with the 'adaptive' options, which directly tackle problems and attempt to resolve them.

Given their popularity, it is not surprising to find many, many variations on the avoidance and escape coping strategies. Examples include ignoring situations, minimizing those situations that *are* recognized, detachment, withdrawal, and even downright denial. If we take this chapter's focus of physical health as an example, avoidance and escape coping would include such things as passively accepting that a broken bone marked the end of a physically active lifestyle. It would mean withdrawing from the places and the people that were part of a more active lifestyle and accepting a restricted, more limited range of activity. It would also include variations in denying this restriction, if others were to press you to resume a more active lifestyle. Specific examples include diverting attention away from this topic in conversation or 'intellectualization' of the difficulty. This includes ways of thinking and talking about a more restricted and limited physical lifestyle by reference to facts or theories that bamboozle the listener, and allow the speaker to maintain their avoidance and escape.

So far, I have indicated that escape and avoidance coping is inevitably maladaptive. However, there can be situations where such forms of coping are for the best. At least in the short term, when faced with an event that is truly beyond our power to influence, then it may be adaptive for us to minimize, through various escape and avoidance strategies, the extent that we have to deal with such an unmanageable stressor.

Classic examples include caring for somebody who has a terminal or long-term illness, such as a dementia. As there are no known ways of resolving a dementia (although there are important ways of limiting its impact and improving the sufferer's quality of life), it is therefore futile and self-harming to engage inappropriately in attempts to resolve such a disease. In a practical sense, then, things like respite care is an explicit form of escape coping that we would all endorse. If nothing else, such coping allows the carer to regain their strength for a further stint of caring. We might also say that the carer is entitled to a break and to opportunities to enjoy their own life more fully.

Therefore, although in general the use of avoidance and escape-coping strategies is questionable, there are circumstances where they may be the best option. If nothing else, we can probably all recognize right now some areas of our life that we are handling by avoidance and escape, perhaps in order to allow us to focus our more adaptive coping strategies on other priorities. In this sense, avoidance and escape may give us a sense of perspective and some thinking time to prepare us for the eventual engagement with the troublesome event in our life. We can also think of some of the different specific coping strategies as varying in how maladaptive they are. To minimize a threat and withdraw somewhat from a very stressful part of our life is rather different from totally ignoring or denying the very existence of a problem. One of the fundamental problems that I have noted earlier in this book with regard to excessive avoidance and escape is that we are not acknowledging that something has ended. A common reaction with losses of various kinds, including the loss of our physical prowess, is to fantasize and to deny. These things do not help us to accept that something has ended – and if we cannot recognize an ending, then it is not possible to begin a transition. Like the ostrich, avoidance and escape-based coping will leave us stuck in the sand. Although removing our head from the sand may result in a period of disorientation and confusion that we would rather avoid, this stage of 'lostness' is actually necessary for us to make a successful transition.

### '*Automatic' escape – the example of 'numbing'*

Just as some conscious efforts to escape can be valuable, so at times we are helped by 'unconscious' forms of escape. A good example is the commonly reported experience of psychological 'numbing' that usually accompanies a traumatic event. This numbing cocoons us, protecting us from fully taking in what has happened. It wards off a full realization of the threat that has been posed and reduces the experience of emotional pain.

Early signs of this numbing can be seen in the way that people typically 'freeze', feel 'stunned' or 'dazed' immediately following a very stressful event. What may appear to onlookers like a surprising level of calmness and self-control is actually the emergence of the cocoon of numbness. Related to this may be exaggerated efforts to avoid facing something traumatic, as in drinking heavily, using drugs, travelling, or even the exaggerated use of humour. These serve to help the individual to avoid things that link back to something that is intolerable, whether it is people, places, sights, smells, feelings, etc. Connected to such things may be an inability to remember details of events, and a general loss of interest in everything (including feeling detached or estranged). There may also be a reduced ability to experience feelings properly, or to fully engage with the things around you. All of this has been described as being like a 'robot', of having 'straw' for a brain, of being 'empty'.

Although these experiences are unwelcome, they can be seen as the brain's automatic 'defence mechanism'. They do, after all, make sense – giving us enough capacity to get by, but without placing our vulnerable selves at further immediate risk. In time (approximately two to three years, depending on the actual event), the cocoon begins to erode and we 're-discover' our selves. We are no longer so vulnerable and we are ready to get on with our lives.

## *Catharsis*

A step on from avoidance and escape is the expression or ventilation of emotions. Again, we humans have a bewildering range of specific coping strategies that we can use to facilitate catharsis. These include tears, tantrums, black humour, 'acting out', and the open criticism of people held responsible for our predicament. Expressing our emotions in these ways will usually help to reduce unpleasant sensations such as tension, anxiety or frustration.

Many of the books that deal with the mid-life crisis draw on one particularly powerful way of facilitating catharsis: this is self-help groups, which enable fellow sufferers to exchange stories about their experience. Not only do such groups help the participants to 'off-load' weighty emotional material, they also tend to give them a sense of acceptance or validation via the other members of the group. Building on the general experience of off-loading feelings, other people in a group can also help an individual to become more aware and descriptive of their emotions, something that is necessary in order to move on successfully. A vague feeling can become teased out into two or three overlapping emotions, and these may be tracked down to two or three different kinds of problems in someone's life. Such clarification or problem definition allows us to more intelligently choose how to cope.

A more spectacular – and at times puzzling – example of emotional-discharge coping is the various ways that people 'act out'. This can include mid-life, securely married people suddenly becoming promiscuous, experimenting with drugs, or taking to such seemingly alien activities as shoplifting. Although these seem to be completely different kinds of activity, they may all serve to reduce emotional discomfort. Again, we have to see past the specific form of somebody's activity to its function – in other words, we have to ask how behaving or feeling in this way helps you to adapt.

### *Emotional support*

As the catharsis example of a self-help group illustrates, social support is integral to emotional coping. Not only do we need people in order to make sense of our feelings, we also need people to help us to deal with our emotions and to give us emotional support. One of the most unsettling emotions we can experience, in fact, is that of being isolated from or abandoned by others. Conversely, to be

95

embraced and supported by others is vital for our emotional health, and it follows that emotion-based coping strategies that encourage others to support us are priceless. That is, as opposed to denying feelings or minimizing them, we encourage social support by an appropriate degree of disclosure. If we let others into our private world of emotions, they will normally respond supportively. This is an extremely delicate coping strategy, though, and requires what has been called 'emotional intelligence'. This is our ability to understand the needs, moods and motives of others – our ability to grasp the social situation and pick up on subtle cues. A lack of emotional intelligence may result in others retreating or even attacking us for our emotional disclosures. However, exercising emotional intelligence will greatly strengthen a relationship. This is because it builds on the fundamental human need for social approval and interaction.

In some respects this emotional intelligence can be thought of as something that is innate, and no doubt some aspects of how we cope emotionally are given to us at birth. This includes our ability to attend closely to what other people are saying and to show through facial expressions and so forth an appropriate response. But there are surely also areas of our emotional intelligence that can be developed through practice. If you think about it, counsellors and therapists are cases in point. Although selected for training on the basis of some innate emotional intelligence, such as the ability to understand or empathize with others, they are also given lengthy periods of training to either strengthen these innate skills or to add fresh ones. An example of such a skill is the ability to disentangle reflexes physiological states from true emotions, as touched on at the beginning of this chapter. As a result of such an improved understanding, therapists are often able to help people to develop their emotional coping strategies, along the lines that will be illustrated in the next couple of sections. For now, a good example is the one of 'anger management training'. This explicit approach to developing emotional coping teaches the pupil to better recognize and manage the different stages of anger arousal.

### Managing emotions

Anger management and the skilful use of social support help us to regulate our emotions. There are, though, some other very general methods that should be mentioned before we go on to discuss further techniques. By 'general methods' I mean the need to give ourselves a firm platform for dealing with transition in an effective emotional way. This includes adequate rest and sleep, as mentioned previously, having an appropriate emotional balance between negative and positive feelings, being reasonably tolerant or accepting of distress, and having a sufficiently healthy lifestyle, including exercise and a sound diet. I stress these general factors because not only can they cause emotional problems if mismanaged, but they will also undermine our ability to cope emotionally.

The first step in managing our emotions successfully is awareness. Despite the central place that our emotions have within our lives, we are often stunningly out of touch with how we feel. Not only are we unable to accurately describe or label our emotions, but we are also often unable to pick out differences in the strength of the different emotions.

To give you a clinical example, it is normal to find people quite unable to pinpoint their level of physical tension. I have even treated a man who was wrongly convinced that he had had a heart attack, and was unable to see that he was experiencing any form of tension at all. The doctors who first treated him found no sign whatsoever of a heart attack, indicating that psychological factors were probably at work. However, the man flatly denied experiencing any tension in his body. It was only when, with the help of a 'biofeedback' machine (this is an electronic device that provides an auditory or visual signal about our level of muscular tension), that he began to realize that he was experiencing very high levels of tension. Later on in therapy, he was able to accept that the chest pains that he had been experiencing were not, after all, necessarily due to a heart attack. This improved awareness created the basis for his recovery.

You can buy biofeedback machines or 'relaxometers' in the shops for a modest sum, and these can provide a valuable way of develop-ing your awareness of physical tension and general arousal. Another more traditional approach is to use such methods as muscular relaxation, yoga and meditation. There are a number of ways to practise relaxation (see the end of this chapter). The essence is to spend some quiet time focusing your attention on the contrasting feelings of tension and relaxation as you work through the different muscle groups of your body. This process will eventually transform your ability to notice – and control – changes in your level of tension and associated arousal. This often lies at the heart of anxiety-related problems, such as difficulties in public situations. With practice, and particularly by using variable cues to relaxation such as breathing out, we can develop our ability to cope through our emotional arousal.

By heightening our awareness of our arousal levels, we therefore create the possibility of managing how we feel. If we succeed, we can spend more of our time in what athletes call the 'zone of optimal functioning'. This is the state in between too little arousal and too much. When we are under-aroused we will tend to make errors, be clumsy and under-achieve. But there are dangers in going too far in the other direction, because over-arousal will tend to cause us to think poorly and be easily distracted, resulting in bad decision-making. The zone in the middle is called optimal because it allows us to function at the peak of our abilities. And by developing our ability to use relaxation techniques, we are better able to know that we are out of this zone and to manoeuvre ourselves back into it.

The final example of managing our emotions that I wish to highlight is the importance of developing a balanced emotional approach. We can cope more effectively in an emotional way by having a reasonable balance between an awareness of our negative emotions (such as excessive attention or arousal) and our more positive ones. In this way, by switching our attention away from something that is causing a negative emotion to something that is causing a more positive affect, we can gain some perspective and relief.

There are at least three ways in which positive emotions can help us to cope:

- to give us a breather or distraction from a negative emotion or event
- to boost or sustain our positive sense of who we are or how we are handling a situation
- as a way of restoring and reconnecting us to positive events or helpful people

### Emotional 'working through'

The main contrast with the ostrich-like use of avoidance and escape is 'working through' an emotion or a problem. Instead of being preoccupied with negative feelings or ruminating on something that has gone wrong, or instead of a resigned acceptance of one's situation, in working through one tries to find ways to accept and overcome difficulties.

To continue from the example of relaxation training, one way to work through an emotion is to tackle the source of the discomfort directly. In therapy circles, terms such as 'graded exposure' and 'desensitization' are used to capture this sense of working through a problem. In such treatments, an individual who may be phobic or extremely anxious is helped to face up to their fear in a gradual, manageable way. This may include initial training in how to relax, leading on to imagining a problematic situation or object (e.g. being in the dentist's chair). Only when the individual is able to cope with the situation in their imagination are they moved on to dealing with it in real life. The exposure approach gradually encourages someone to deal with a feared situation, with the result that they discover several things of value. Partly, exposure helps us to realize that some of our worst fears are without foundation. As many people have noted, it is not the fear or negative emotion itself that is so upsetting, but rather the fear of what this might lead to. Such unhelpful imaginings are tested out through exposure and almost always falsified (e.g. the fear that if you panic and do not escape, you will go mad or have a heart attack).

To return to the example of our physical well-being, working through might mean accepting some limitation on our physical ability and re-focusing our efforts on other, compensatory aspects of our selves. In this way, someone who feels keenly the loss of athletic prowess may find solace in developing other, more emotional, ways of relating to others. Examples include developing your creative, intuitive or nurturant side. Just as exposure treatment can falsify some irrational beliefs, so can a transition to a more emotional way of functioning help us to realize that there are other successful ways of 'being', in addition to such things as physical prowess.

In general, then, working through something emotionally is about progressing from avoidance to active and purposeful engagement with the challenge of transition. As noted, this involves the necessary initial step of accepting that change is necessary. It then includes the energy to take the first steps towards making change a reality. Instead of resigned acceptance, we need to grasp the nettle, as illustrated by Teena's account:

99

*I was ready to move on and one of the things I did was to clear out a whole pile of stuff from my bureau. There were photos, and while they were there they were an anchor to the past, to when I was happy. The nursery photos, the house, the winter walks – all my life was in that drawer. I even once spent the whole night looking at them and didn't want to move on. I had one foot in that past life.*

*But one day I felt ready to move on. I had one final look at all the photos and then boxed them up. This helped get rid of some of the anger and made me more ready to commit to a new life. I realized that the old one was over, was behind me. It was a big thing, the end of all that.*

One way of thinking about this working-through process is in terms of 'fighting spirit'. Particularly in relation to the treatment of life-threatening illnesses, there is reason to believe that those who react with a fighting spirit, rather than by denial, are those who do best. People with a fighting spirit believe they have the ability to fight back, to conquer, and ultimately recover from their illness. They do not simply stoically accept their condition or feel helpless or hopeless. As a result of this fighting spirit, they will then engage in the relevant coping behaviours, such as seeking information and enlisting social support. Other examples of this coping spirit would include taking more exercise and generally improving your lifestyle (eating less and eating better, getting adequate rest). The following example, provided by Mike, illustrates this 'lifestyle' approach:

*I felt a strong need to give myself a fighting chance in grappling with my problems. For me, this meant getting myself fit – so I joined a sports club and made a point of taking vigorous exercise three or four times a week. Although I really had to drag myself there most evenings, I was rewarded. I soon started to feel physically better in myself and my sense of being in control was improved. Another thing that I got from exercise was a sense of perspective, particularly when going for a jog in the countryside. There is something about getting out into nature that helps to put your problems in perspective.*

This quote indicates fighting spirit allied to a particular coping strategy: the use of exercise to strengthen our ability to process problems in an emotional way.

## Points to Ponder

- A wide range of common emotions are listed in the box on page 89. Have another look at this and see if you can identify, from your own experience, emotions that you have felt during your crisis period. Can you also recognize situations that tend to cause you to feel these emotions?
- The various types of emotional coping were picked out at the beginning of this chapter. Can you align yourself with any of these approaches?
- And perhaps of most value, can you 'personalize' the five forms of emotional coping that are listed above (i.e. make them as relevant to your needs as possible)?

## Things to Try

If you are able to recognize your coping 'profile' in relation to the list of five emotional coping strategies (see pages 91–2), then the next step is to logically consider how you might take one of these and progress it. In other words, in relation to a particular problem (which might itself be a negative emotion such as anxiety), can you recognize the value of one of the five coping strategies and tweak it so that it is something you can try out? The other major thing that you may wish to try is the progressive muscular relaxation approach, as touched on in the section on managing emotions. You may also find it helpful to purchase a relaxation cassette or CD. A related option is to join a yoga or meditation class, as these will also help to heighten your self-awareness of emotional functioning and will promote your ability to cope emotionally.

# 7

# Conclusion

You are free to do whatever you like. You need only face the consequences.

(Sheldon Kopp, 1974)

It is now time to draw this guide to coping with a mid-life crisis to a conclusion. We need to reflect on what has been covered, and form a picture of what remains to be done. If life is akin to sailing the seven seas, then are we now safely berthed and ready for the next stage?

In doing this review, we need to re-focus from a preoccupation with whatever may have gone wrong or have upset us. Instead of being bound up by all kinds of unfavourable comparisons, regrets or idealizations of how life should have been, we need to firm up our new coping strategies and step forth on our journey towards personal growth and well-being.

## *Correct faulty assumptions*

Perhaps this review can best be started by comparing some of the fundamental assumptions that most of us tend to make. One key assumption we may have made is that we are somehow safe, that bad things simply will not happen to us. As those who have the misfortune to be involved in traumatic events can confirm, the reality is that we are *all* vulnerable, and so all sorts of things can happen to us: our personal 'armour' is an illusion. However, this is not to preach apathy or resignation, but rather to encourage the development of rational beliefs and the living of each day to the full. Another error we can make is the opposite of this belief: that because something traumatic has happened to us in the past, it is bound to happen again. It seems to me that a more rational belief is that, if you take reasonable care through coping appropriately, the probability of something traumatic happening is reduced to a level that allows you to live a full and satisfying life. But just to be sure, we should live each day as if it were our last – or at least strive to!

Invest your efforts in what you really believe to matter. Life is too short for more of the same.

A second major assumption that many people tend to make is that the world is basically a safe, orderly and predictable place – which clearly it isn't. Again, being the victim of some terrible event will quickly undermine or 'de-stabilize' this assumption and require us to form more realistic beliefs. For instance, it is in fact a *sound* belief that the world is a dangerous place – as crime and terrorism make plain. It certainly can be chaotic and unpredictable too. Adopting appropriate coping strategies, such as setting modest, achievable goals that are under our control, is sensible in the light of this. Just because things are chaotic, though, does not mean that we have no control. Similarly, assuming that something will probably go wrong (or at least that our ideal outcome may not be attainable) may alleviate much of the stress that comes with modern living.

A final major assumption that nearly all of us tend to make is that we are 'good' people. It is far harder to accept that we each have elements of 'badness' in us. Are you always 100 per cent decent and worthy? Accepting that we are less than perfect is not to diminish our self-esteem, but instead will help us to adopt a more balanced, tolerant self-appraisal. Just because we are not perfect doesn't mean that we are all bad. There are many good things that we can do and which we probably do more frequently than we realize. Also, just because something bad may have happened to us, it doesn't mean that we are bad people – many events are simply the unfolding of random chains of activity. We just get caught up in things that are not of our doing. So be sure to apportion responsibility appropriately – focus on what is good and strong and valued in yourself, taking responsibility and credit for that.

At this point I am keenly aware that many topics and angles relating to the mid-life crisis have not been covered, and there is simply not enough space in this short book to tackle the many important issues that inevitably have been omitted (or at least under-emphasized). For instance, what about those fascinating and important differences between men and women? Research and clinical experience teaches us that these differences can be marked, and that they operate in fascinating ways. For example, men and women need social support in different ways, and they also use it differently. As a result, while a man benefits from having a close confiding partner on whom to off-load his angst, commonly the woman suffers as a result. Men tend not to be so willing or able in the way that they reciprocate such social support. Similar interesting tales could be told about many of the other issues covered within this book.

By way of my own personal 'closure', I have been much influenced by reading the biography of Billy Connolly. This ends with 'Billy's desiderata', a re-working of the much-cited desiderata written originally by Max Ehrmann. Both spell out things that are desired, a philosophy on how best to lead your life. Inspired by these examples, and as a way of summarizing the 'seven Cs' that form the chapter titles and philosophy within this book, I close by offering you my own 'desiderata'. It is the summary of my advice, which I hope will assist you on your own journey onward from a mid-life crisis:

*Go purposefully through your crisis, keeping all things in perspective. Cultivate a sense of objectivity about your turmoil, an ability to gain 'distance', and so exercise your wisdom during the times of transition. For although there may be turmoil, you need not be the turmoil. Then you can usefully get started, which is first of all to recognize what has stopped. Before we can make any progress, there needs to be an end to what has held us back. 'In our end is our beginning'. We are all distinctive players on life's stage, creatures shaped uniquely from our beginning. So be keenly aware of who you are. Heighten this self-awareness, for it is your essence and your only true guide. Try to develop a similar understanding and compassion for those around you, especially the people you love. Recognize too how people and places shape you and mould how you change, for we are often steered away from who we are and where we would be by circumstances. Do not be cynical or waste your energy on trying to fix the past. Refocus. Aim to stay 'positively preoccupied'. Engage with the people who will support you, trusting your plan. They deserve your time and energy. Cherish them and draw on them to overcome your lifetraps, those self-defeating, recurring patterns with which we all struggle. Harness them to your chariot of personal transition, following your path to a stronger, more contented place. 'You can run, but you can't hide'. So, it is necessary to adapt. Following this path means making sense of what has happened, and along the way confronting stark, uncomfortable realities in you and in life itself. The world is not as we assume it to be. Strive to keep your strong emotions within your 'comfort zone' as you go, accepting as inevitable and necessary those unpleasant feelings that accompany significant personal transformation. Like the seasons, they should all be experienced. Try to turn them to your purpose, like the following wind. Through it all, maintain belief and hope. There is a way, and you can travel it with skill and flair. You know this to be true, for you have travelled a path like this before. There is no doubt that you have many competencies, and people admire you for these and will respect your resolve. As you follow your path you need to work through so much that has held you back and blighted your past happiness. Deal openly and collaboratively with these problems, for others feel your pain and share your hopes. Your friends can nurture you when your journey pauses, guiding you with information and aiding you with their help. Along the way, take time to refresh and strengthen yourself, as much that feels wrong is nothing more than tiredness and loneliness. Return the love of those who support you, to strengthen your sense of belonging and purpose. There is much ground to travel, but when you reach the end of this path you will be 're-invented', transformed to a design of your own making. Undoubtedly, much still remains to be done, as you now see new paths, ones that draw you on to your next journey. These are paths towards truth and they promise you greater well-being. But pause first to enjoy the place you have reached, for you have come far and shown huge self-belief. So, be happy with yourself as you journey on, for you have made it all worthwhile.*

# Further reading

Bridges, William (1980) *Transitions: Making Sense of Life's Changes*, Perseus Books.

Brown, G. and Harris, T. (1978) *Social Origins of Depression*, Tavistock.

Erikson, Erik (1950) *Childhood and Society*, Norton.

Gallwey, T. (1975) *The Inner Game of Tennis*, Pan. (You don't need to be interested in tennis to find what is important in this book, although Gallwey has also written 'inner game' accounts of golf, skiing and business.)

Garland, Jeff and Christina (2001) *Life Review in Health and Social Care*, Brunner-Routledge.

Kopp, Sheldon (1974) *If You Meet the Buddha on the Road, Kill Him*, Sheldon Press.

Lazarus, R. S. and B. N. (1994) *Passion and Reason: Making Sense of Our Emotions*, Oxford University Press.

Miller, William, and de Baca, Janet C' (2001) *Quantum Change*, Guilford Press.

Rutter, M. (1978) 'Human growth and development', in Jerome S. Bruner and Alison Garton, eds, *Human Growth and Development*, Wolfsen College Lectures, Clarendon Press.

Sheehy, Gail (1976) *Passages*, Bantam Press.

Young, Jeffrey, and Klosko, Janet (1994) *Re-inventing Your Life*, Penguin Books.

# Index